Hiking Colorado's Uncompahgre Wilderness

Help Us Keep This Guide Up to Date

Every effort has been made by the author and editors to make this guide as accurate and useful as possible. However, many things can change after a guide is published—trails are rerouted, regulations change, techniques evolve, facilities come under new management, etc.

We would love to hear from you concerning your experiences with this guide and how you feel it could be improved and kept up to date. While we may not be able to respond to all comments and suggestions, we'll take them to heart and we'll also make certain to share them with the author. Please send your comments and suggestions to the following address:

The Globe Pequot Press
Reader Response/Editorial Department
P.O. Box 480
Guilford, CT 06437

Or you may e-mail us at:

editorial@GlobePequot.com

Thanks for your input, and happy travels!

Hiking Colorado's Uncompahgre Wilderness

William B. Crick

FALCON®

GUILFORD, CONNECTICUT
HELENA, MONTANA
AN IMPRINT OF THE GLOBE PEQUOT PRESS

A **FALCON** GUIDE ®

Maps created by XNR Productions Inc. © The Globe Pequot
Press

Library of Congress Cataloging-in-Publication Data
Crick, William B.
  Hiking Colorado's Uncompahgre Wilderness / William
B. Crick.—1st ed.
      p. cm. — (A Falcon Guide)
  ISBN 0-7627-1109-4
  1. Hiking—Colorado—Uncompahgre National Forest—
Guidebooks. 2. Trails—Colorado—Uncompahgre na-
tional Forest—Guidebooks. 3. Uncompahgre National
Forest (Colo.)—Guidebook. I. Title. II. Series.

GV199.42.C62U543 2003
917.88'25—dc21   2003048050

Manufactured in the United States of America
First Edition/First Printing

Contents

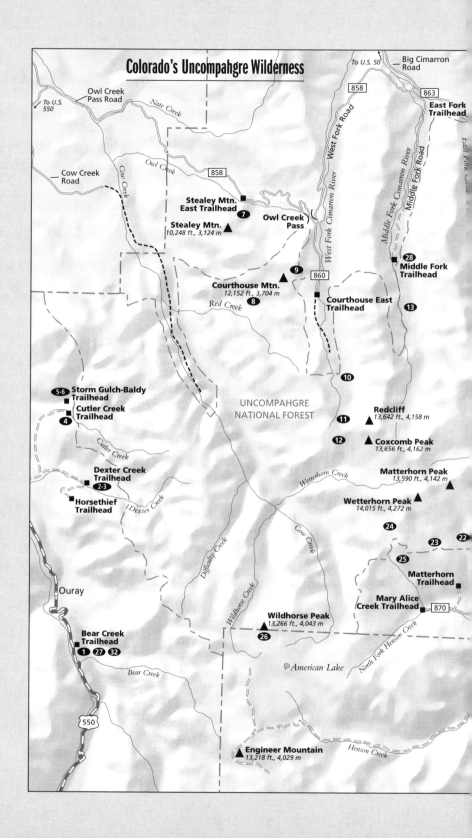

Colorado's Uncompahgre Wilderness

To U.S. 50 — Big Cimarron Road

To U.S. 550

Owl Creek Pass Road

Nate Creek

858

863

East Fork Trailhead

Cow Creek Road

Owl Creek

858

Stealey Mtn. East Trailhead **7**

Owl Creek Pass

Stealey Mtn.
10,248 ft., 3,124 m ▲

Courthouse Mtn.
12,152 ft., 3,704 m ▲ **9**

860

28 Middle Fork Trailhead

Red Creek **8**

Courthouse East Trailhead

13

West Fork Road

West Fork Cimarron River

Middle Fork Cimarron River

Middle Fork Road

East Fork Cimar...

10

Storm Gulch-Baldy Trailhead **5-6**

Cutler Creek Trailhead **4**

Cutler Creek

UNCOMPAHGRE NATIONAL FOREST

11 Redcliff
13,642 ft., 4,158 m ▲

12 ▲ Coxcomb Peak
13,656 ft., 4,162 m

Dexter Creek Trailhead **2-3**

Dexter Creek

Horsethief Trailhead ■

Wetterhorn Creek

Matterhorn Peak
13,590 ft., 4,142 m ▲

Wetterhorn Peak ▲
14,015 ft., 4,272 m

24

23 **22**

25

Matterhorn Trailhead ■

Cow Creek

Difficulty Creek

Wildhorse Creek

Ouray

Mary Alice Creek Trailhead

870

Bear Creek Trailhead
1 **27** **32**

Wildhorse Peak
13,266 ft., 4,043 m ▲
26

North Fork Henson Creek

American Lake

Bear Creek

550

Engineer Mountain ▲
13,218 ft., 4,029 m

Henson Creek

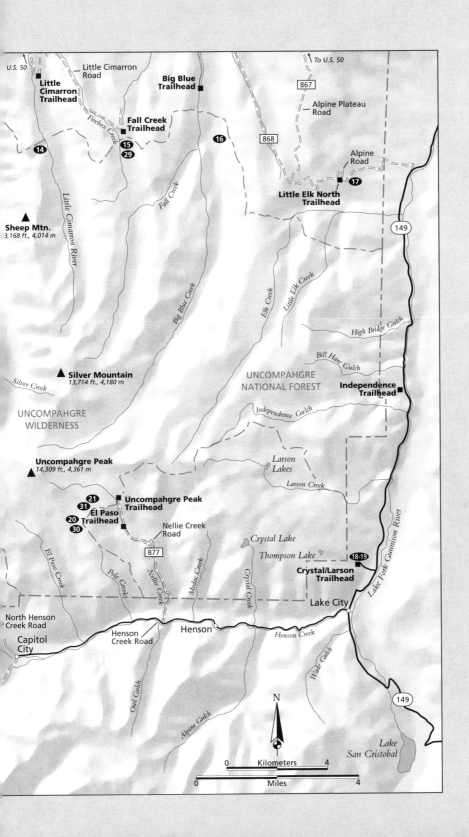

U.S. 50

Little Cimarron Road

Big Blue Trailhead ■

To U.S. 50 ↑

867

Little Cimarron Trailhead ■

Firebox Creek

Fall Creek Trailhead

Alpine Plateau Road

868

14

15
29

16

Alpine Road

Fall Creek

17

Little Elk North Trailhead ■

Little Cimarron River

▲ **Sheep Mtn.**
3,168 ft., 4,014 m

149

Big Blue Creek

Elk Creek

Little Elk Creek

High Bridge Gulch

Bill Hare Gulch

▲ **Silver Mountain**
13,714 ft., 4,180 m

UNCOMPAHGRE NATIONAL FOREST

Independence Trailhead ■

Silver Creek

Independence Gulch

UNCOMPAHGRE WILDERNESS

Larson Lakes

Uncompahgre Peak
14,309 ft., 4,361 m ▲

Larson Creek

21
31

Uncompahgre Peak Trailhead ■

20
30

El Paso Trailhead ■

Nellie Creek Road

Crystal Lake

Lake Fork Gunnison River

El Paso Creek

Pole Creek

877

Nellie Creek

Modoc Creek

Crystal Creek

Thompson Lake

18-19

Crystal/Larson Trailhead

Lake City

North Henson Creek Road

Henson Creek Road

Henson

Henson Creek

Capitol City

Owl Gulch

Alpine Gulch

Wade Gulch

149

N

Lake San Cristobal

0   Kilometers   4

0   Miles   4

Backpacks

Map Legend

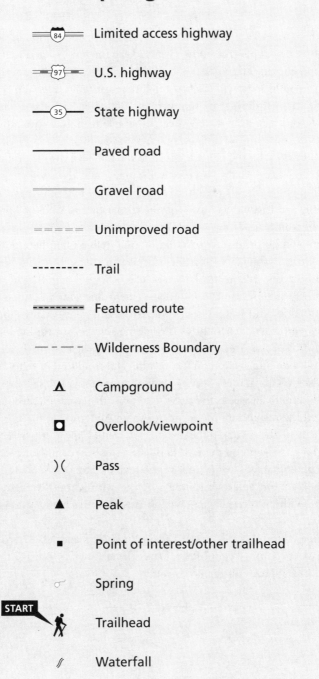

Limited access highway

U.S. highway

State highway

Paved road

Gravel road

Unimproved road

Trail

Featured route

Wilderness Boundary

Campground

Overlook/viewpoint

Pass

Peak

Point of interest/other trailhead

Spring

Trailhead

Waterfall

Acknowledgments

My wife, Cathy Crick, deserves much credit for the completion of this book. Her encouragement and positive attitude helped keep the research and writing process moving along at many stages. Without her watchful eye I might never have been aware that this opportunity with Falcon Publishing existed. Cathy also spent many of her valuable days off during the summers of 2000 and 2001 accompanying me on the trails of the Uncompahgre. She helped me maintain a positive attitude when I was suffering a severe stomach illness one night at Slide Lake and carried more than her share of the load on the difficult return to the trailhead the next morning. Toward the end of the process, Cathy also reviewed the text and maps for accuracy and content, providing invaluable suggestions to improve the manuscript.

Cathy and I would like to thank the owners of the Western Motel on East Main Street in Montrose. They softened the difficulties of being on the road with their kindness and hospitality. If you'd like a comfortable night before or after an outing in the Uncompahgre, we recommend that you check in at the Western.

Without the willing and able assistance of several members of the USDA Forest Service, the U.S. Bureau of Land Management, and Ouray Trails, the job of producing an accurate and useful book would have been considerably more difficult. Louis French, who works in Montrose as wilderness supervisor for the Uncompahgre and Sneffels Wilderness Areas, was supportive of the project from its inception and provided valuable information on the location and condition of trails. Greg Austin, trails supervisor for the Forest Service in Gunnison, provided valuable information on trail conditions, answered the many questions that were pitched to him, and twice reviewed the manuscript for accuracy. Arden Anderson of the U.S. Bureau of Land Management also reviewed the manuscript. Dan Hippe accompanied me for a wonderful long weekend on the East Fork and Horsethief Trails and provided a number of fine photographs. The manuscript was reviewed by Bob Value and Joe Leiper, both published authors and rock climbing friends with whom I've shared adventures for decades. Without their able and willing assistance, this book would be a much lesser product.

Three editors, Jay Nichols at Falcon Publishing and Jeff Serena and David Singleton of The Globe Pequot Press, helped in many ways to make the process enjoyable and to improve this guide's quality.

Introduction

The San Juan Mountains of southwestern Colorado are a land of soaring peaks, widespread plateaus, and deep lush valleys as remote and undeveloped as any area in the Rocky Mountains. It is a spectacular natural area that includes mountain peaks, large areas of alpine tundra, year-round snowfields, hot springs, spruce-fir and aspen subalpine forests, high lakes, snow-fed creeks, and abundant wildlife. Since the mid-1800s extensive mineral deposits have been exploited, and more recently residential development has begun climbing the slopes of the San Juans. In the process the San Juans have been carved into smaller undeveloped parcels. A few of the larger parcels have been protected as wilderness areas, including the Uncompahgre Wilderness.

Located in the north-central San Juan Mountains, the Uncompahgre Wilderness extends to the north from a line roughly connecting the towns of Ouray and Lake City, Colorado. The wilderness includes 110 miles of managed hiking trails and many more miles of hikeable terrain spread over its 102,668 acres. Nearly the entire area is higher than 10,000 feet above sea level; two fourteeners and at least twenty-five peaks above 13,000 feet pierce the sky in the Uncompahgre. The northern and eastern parts of the area feature lofty but often gentle north-to-south-trending ridges resembling the fingers of the human hand, separated by drainages associated with the various forks of the Cimarron River and other tributaries to the Gunnison River lying to the north. The southern and western portions of the Uncompahgre are largely alpine and above timberline, with high plateaus and rugged, glacier-cut peaks. Because more than half of the Uncompahgre Wilderness is more than 11,000 feet above sea level, a relatively high level of physical fitness is required to hike in the area. The Uncompahgre is not nearly as large and imposing as the nearby Weminuche Wilderness, however. In one day of hiking you can be in the most remote parts of the Uncompahgre, and it can be crossed in a north-south direction by any of several routes in only a day or two.

Many types of wildlife prosper in the Uncompahgre Wilderness. Forested areas are inhabited by snowshoe hares, mule deer, elk, mountain lions, bobcats, black bears, and coyotes; areas above timberline hold abundant pikas, marmots, ptarmigans, and occasional herds of bighorn sheep. Many of these animals are rarely encountered by hikers, but deer, elk, pikas, and marmots can often be counted on to enliven your wilderness experience. Large herds of elk live in certain remote areas of the Uncompahgre, where their behavior in the occasional presence of humans will attest to their desire for quiet.

The Uncompahgre Wilderness is managed by the USDA Forest Service. The area is split between two Forest Service districts, with the line running generally north-northeast along ridgelines. The area west of the boundary is managed by the Ouray Ranger District based in Montrose, and the area east of the boundary is managed by

the Gunnison Ranger District in Gunnison. A small part of the southwestern Uncompahgre Wilderness between Engineer Pass and American Flats is managed by the Bureau of Land Management. For information contact the Ouray Ranger District and BLM offices at 2505 South Townsend, Montrose, CO 81401, phone (970) 240–5300, www.fs.fed.us/r2/gmug; or the Gunnison Ranger District, 216 North Colorado, Gunnison, CO 81230, phone (970) 641–0471.

This guide is intended to describe the "system" (officially recognized) trails in the Uncompahgre, as well as a handful of high-quality, off-trail peak hikes. This book is intended to help make your visit one that you will always remember.

Hiking in the Uncompahgre

The Uncompahgre is not an exceptionally large wilderness area; at just over 100,000 acres, it is only the thirteenth largest wilderness area in Colorado. As such the Uncompahgre is more accessible than many wilderness areas; in only a few weeks of hiking, I was able to gain a fairly intimate knowledge of the area's layout. The Uncompahgre, like many Colorado wilderness areas, lies in a very high mountain setting. Most trailheads lie between 8,500 and 10,500 feet, and on many trails you will be gaining elevation with your first steps. The distances involved in getting deep into the Uncompahgre are not great, but the high elevations and steep gradients will ensure that you get your exercise even on the more moderate day hikes.

Also because of high elevations, the hiking season in the Uncompahgre centers around the summer months. In years following a dry winter, all trails will be passable by early June, but more typically it is at least late June before the high country fully melts out. Late May is a wonderful time to hike the lower elevations of the Uncompahgre. The Baldy, Storm Gulch, Cutler Creek Loop, and Little Elk Trails, as well as lower reaches of many other trails, are suitable for this time of year. Higher areas are accessible to adventurous souls who put out the extra effort of carrying snowshoes or skis; early in the season the large snowfields remaining above timberline add to an already overwhelming beauty. Note that in springtime in the San Juans, occasional heavy snowstorms and prolonged rainy periods can occur; this is the wettest season on average in the Rocky Mountains. Even during fair weather, be prepared for freezing temperatures at night during the spring months.

June and early July in the Uncompahgre often bring clear, warm weather with cool nights and relatively little rainfall, although afternoon and evening thunderstorms are unpredictable and can occur on almost any day. The creeks and rivers will be running high until at least the end of June in a normal summer as the deep winter snowpack melts out, and stream crossings can be difficult. Trails may be more difficult to negotiate due to fallen trees and areas of remaining snow. Heading into July

◀ *Looking down the East Fork Valley.*

warmer weather tends to prevail, at least until the monsoon season arrives in mid- to late July and August. The monsoon is caused by a persistent flow of moist, sub- tropical air northward out of New Mexico and into the high country of southern Colorado. Thunderstorms often develop early in the day during the monsoon, and all-day rainfall events are not uncommon. Perfectly clear days are relatively few dur- ing this time. Hiking during the monsoon season can be enjoyable (particularly for displaced easterners like myself, who carry full rain gear and are accustomed to long periods in the tent) if you are prepared and able to stay dry, as the creeks run strong and the high meadows of wildflowers are at their spectacular best. Try to hike early in the morning, and be prepared to wait out the inevitable afternoon and evening storms. As during the springtime, be prepared for difficult stream crossings during the monsoon season. Note that the monsoon brings moisture from the south and southwest; clouds moving from these directions early in the day almost always signal trouble a few hours later, while summer weather coming from the west and north- west often is good news for the hiker.

In most years the monsoon begins to expire in late August, and around Labor Day begins perhaps the finest time to hike in the Uncompahgre. Crystal-clear, cold nights and warm, sunny days prevail in September and into October. The meadow grasses turn brown while the oak brush and willow, aspen, and cottonwood trees take on the colors that draw hundreds of thousands of viewers every year to the Col- orado mountains. The peak hikes described in this book are less crowded in fall de- spite this stable weather pattern. Be aware, however, that early-season snowstorms can occur (particularly during October), requiring that you be properly equipped. Daylight hours are short and the nights are long, so plan shorter days in fall than you would during the middle of summer. By sometime in late October into November, the first snows begin to settle into the high country; the same lower-elevation trails that make good springtime hikes are also suitable now, but the higher trails begin to build their annual snowpack. By early December in all but the driest years, you'll find that any hiking in the Uncompahgre involves extensive slogging. Wintertime use of the area is extremely difficult, as many trailheads are not accessible by vehicle.

Topographic Maps and Finding the Trail

The entire Uncompahgre Wilderness is covered on Trails Illustrated Map 141, titled "Silverton, Ouray, Telluride, Lake City." This map is published at a scale of 1:66,667 (a little more than 1 inch per mile) and is widely available at outdoor equipment stores. The Trails Illustrated map is an excellent tool for trip planning, and on famil- iar or uncomplicated ground it may be all you need to carry. The scale is too small, however, to be useful for orienteering, or to predict other than very large variations in terrain. In some areas the accuracy of this map (given the limitations of its scale) is acceptable, while in others (the Independence Trail comes to mind) the map's por- trayal of a route is inaccurate.

Bill Crick at a trail intersection on American Flats. Photo: Dan Hippe

The following United States Geological Survey (USGS) 1:24,000 quads make up a complete set for hiking in the Uncompahgre Wilderness:

Alpine Plateau
Courthouse Mountain
Dallas
Handies Peak
Ironton
Lake City
Ouray
Sheep Mountain
Uncompahgre Peak
Wetterhorn Peak

There are trails in the Uncompahgre that are not marked on the USGS quads, and other trails that are mislocated due to their realignment over the years. This book attempts to point out such conditions, either in the Trail Conditions section or in the body of the trail description.

Certain sections of trail in the Uncompahgre Wilderness have been grown in by vegetation and lack of use or are located in heavily wooded areas without many landmarks. On at least one trail, the very high degree of accuracy of the USGS Courthouse Mountain quadrangle was responsible for my finding the trail and completing the hike. Where a trail seems unclear, I have tried to compensate by increasing the detail of the accompanying trail descriptions. Remember that the Forest Service carries out trail improvement projects each summer, and that the use of a trail may increase or decrease over time. An example is the section of the Horsethief Trail northwest of American Flats, which received trail work in the summer of 2000, and which was very difficult to find prior to that work. As these trail descriptions age, conditions on the ground will change.

Be prepared for a disappearing trail by taking mental and even written notes about landmarks in order to safely reverse your course back to the trailhead. In the Uncompahgre faint trails typically occur in open grassy areas, which can grow over every year. In an open area or meadow where the trail disappears, look first for marker posts, which are commonly placed by the Forest Service to help in trail location. Sometimes the trail through a meadow may be marked simply by a path of slightly shorter grass. Often the only way to deal with a faint trail is to walk the entire perimeter of a meadow, searching for a reappearing trail and/or tree blazes where a trail reenters the trees. Obviously having an idea of where to concentrate the search, using this book and the topographic map, is useful. In areas of spruce-fir forest, typical of elevations between about 9,500 and 11,500 feet in the Uncompahgre, trails stay fresh for a longer period due to relative lack of ground cover.

Although the use of map and compass is beyond the scope of this guide, it is suggested that you gain as much skill as possible prior to venturing into any wilderness area. Wilderness trails may be unmarked or poorly so. Areas that may be easily navigated under clear skies may become very confusing in poor weather, and the consequences of getting lost far from the trailhead can be very serious. Refer to The Globe Pequot Press's concise guide, *Basic Essentials Map and Compass,* or to any of a number of other instructional books. Remember that you alone are responsible for staying "found" when hiking in the Uncompahgre Wilderness.

Access to the Uncompahgre Wilderness

By definition *wilderness* is an area devoid of roads and other human-built structures; therefore wilderness area boundaries may be established close to existing road access points. This is true of the Uncompahgre Wilderness, the edges of which are accessible from twenty-five recognized trailheads. It may be helpful to refer to the Overview Map on page vi when reading this description, which begins near Ouray on the southwest side of the map and works in a clockwise direction.

U.S. Highway 550 runs from south to north through the towns of Silverton, Ouray, Ridgway, and Montrose, providing access to the trailheads on the west side

The view into Difficulty Creek from Horsethief Trail.

of the Uncompahgre Wilderness. From south to north U.S. 550 serves up Bear Creek, Horsethief, Dexter Creek, Cutler Creek, and Storm Gulch/Baldy Trailheads (Hikes 1 through 6). The Owl Creek Pass Road (Ouray County Road 10) leaves U.S. 550 just north of Ridgway and leads to the Stealey Mountain Trail (Hike 7). The Owl Creek Pass Road is also the best approach to the Courthouse (east end), Wetterhorn Basin, Middle Fork, and East Fork Trails for those driving in from the areas around Ouray and Ridgway. Trails beginning in the Cow Creek area (Cow Creek Trail and the west end of the Courthouse Trail) are not described in this book, because a very tricky and difficult stream crossing is necessary to reach them.

Trailheads on the north side of the Uncompahgre Wilderness are accessed via unpaved roads managed mainly by the USDA Forest Service and the Bureau of Land Management. The roads lead south from U.S. Highway 50, which connects the towns of Montrose on the west and Gunnison on the east. The West Fork (Wetterhorn Basin), Courthouse (east), Middle Fork, and East Fork Trailheads are all accessible from the Big Cimarron Road, which leaves U.S. 50 near the settlement of Cimarron, about 21 miles east of Montrose. Just east of the Big Cimarron Road on

U.S. 50 is the turnoff to the Little Cimarron Road, which accesses the Little Cimarron and Fall Creek Trailheads.

Colorado Highway 149 leads south from U.S. 50 (from a point 9 miles west of Gunnison at Blue Mesa Reservoir) to Lake City, Colorado. CO 149 accesses several trailheads (from north to south, the Big Blue Trailhead by way of the Alpine Road, the Independence Trailhead, and the Crystal/Larson Trailhead) on the eastern side of the area. You will also drive CO 149 to Lake City to reach trailheads on the southern side of the Uncompahgre Wilderness. From Lake City take Hinsdale County Road 20, which follows the drainage of Henson Creek west of Lake City and leads to the Nellie Creek and North Henson Creek Roads. The southern trailheads are, in rough east-to-west order, Uncompahgre Peak and El Paso from the Nellie Creek Road, Matterhorn and Mary Alice Creek from the North Henson Creek Road, and finally Horsethief (south end) and the Engineer Pass area.

Most of the trailheads described in this book can be reached by standard passenger cars having an average amount of clearance—at least in good weather and with a few miles of difficult, bumpy driving. For certain trailheads, notably the Courthouse (west end), Stealey Mountain (south end), Uncompahgre Peak, and El Paso, a high-clearance, four-wheel-drive vehicle is an essential piece of equipment. Other trailheads, such as those in the Middle Fork, Big Blue, and Engineer Pass areas, will be more comfortably reached in a high-clearance four-wheel-drive vehicle, but can be reached with careful driving of many passenger cars. Driving conditions are described in detail in the Finding the Trailhead section under each hike, but remember that the condition of the dirt and gravel roads can change from year to year, or even after a single thunderstorm.

Montrose is the nearest town with an airport that supports commercial flights. The fares are expensive, but it is an option. Grand Junction, Colorado, approximately 100 miles from the northwestern edge of the Uncompahgre, has additional commercial flights available. Automobile rental agencies operate out of the area near the Montrose airport, including Budget, Dollar, Enterprise, National, and Thrifty. If you are heading onto some of the rougher roads on the periphery of the Uncompahgre, both Lake City and Ouray have outlets where jeeps can be rented by the day.

Approximate drive times from some major cities to the nearest part of the Uncompahgre Wilderness are given below. Once you are in the area, it can take as much as two additional hours to drive from one trailhead to another, depending on location.

Denver: Five hours to the eastern Uncompahgre via U.S. Highways 285 and 50 through Fairplay and Gunnison; or to the western Uncompahgre via Interstate 70 and U.S. 50 through Grand Junction and Montrose.

Colorado Springs: Four hours via U.S. 50 through Salida and Gunnison.

Albuquerque: Five to six hours.

Phoenix: Seven to eight hours.

Salt Lake City: Six hours.

Backcountry Essentials

Hiking in the high mountain environment has many potential hazards, but with preparation and forethought these can be minimized so that your trips involve only the pleasures. Following the advice in this section of the book will help you not only to survive dangerous situations if they occur, but hopefully to prevent them from developing in the first place. Adverse mountain weather, wildlife encounters, and practicing backcountry etiquette, rather than detracting from your enjoyment, can be among the most rewarding aspects of your trips.

Survival and Comfort

Wilderness travel is generally quite safe (possibly safer than traveling the highways to get there) if you act conservatively and take commonsense precautions. First and foremost, know your limitations and those of your group. Avoid difficult creek crossings, steep or unstable snowfields, rock faces, and other difficult terrain if you are unsure of your group's abilities. Plan your daily hiking distances around your group's physical and mental capabilities. If these capabilities are stretched, it is important to know when to turn around. Be sure to carry enough provisions to survive an extra period of time in the backcountry in case of injury or getting lost. These two precautions will help you avoid most dangerous situations in the wilderness.

When possible, do not travel alone in the wilderness; the fact that you have a companion to seek help in case of injury or other emergency can save your life. If you are traveling alone, keep in mind that even an ankle sprain or a normally minor illness can have serious consequences. Leave a detailed itinerary, map, and expected time of return for your trip with friends or family members. It is highly recommended that you obtain rescue insurance by purchasing a Colorado Hiker's Certificate or hunting or fishing license from the Colorado Division of Wildlife or an outdoor store. Revenue from certificates and licenses helps fund statewide search-and-rescue efforts in Colorado, so purchasing one to cover your outdoor activities is the right thing to do even if you never have to use it.

Do your best to enter the wilderness properly prepared and equipped. Prepare for adverse weather conditions by dressing in layers, with moisture-wicking fabrics next to your skin. For high-mountain hikes be sure you are acclimated. If, as many visitors do, you are coming to the Colorado mountains from a lowland state, spend a couple of days in town or in a campground at lower elevation. Work your way up to higher elevations gradually, and at first for only short periods. Don't skimp on food and water even on day hikes; most cases of altitude sickness are caused primarily by dehydration. Most of all, maintain a sense of humor during the most uncomfortable moments in the backcountry, and chances are that you will survive with a good story to tell.

Treat yourself to as much outdoor education as you can. The more you study and read about wilderness-related topics, the better. Extensive knowledge about mountain weather, nutrition, first aid, orienteering, avalanche safety, ecology, and a host of other topics can only prove useful to you. Even it you never have to pull out the learned skills, they will enhance your enjoyment of the outdoors.

In the Uncompahgre Wilderness or anywhere else in the Rocky Mountains, never drink natural water without first boiling it or passing it through a commercially available filter. Giardia and other parasites are ubiquitous in the backcountry waters of Colorado, and have spoiled many hiking and backpacking outings.

Wildlife

Although encounters with dangerous wildlife are relatively rare in Colorado, it is wise to be prepared for them, and to take certain precautions to try to prevent them. The following is summarized from the books *Bear Aware* and *Mountain Lion Alert,* by Falcon Publishing.

Bears

Hiking in bear country adds a certain unavoidable risk to your trip, but being aware of the possibility will help you avoid the majority of encounters. Always do everything you can to prevent surprising a bear on the trail, and memorize the following five preventive measures:

1. Be alert; see and hear as much as possible on the trail.
2. Don't hike alone.
3. Stay on trails and in open areas.
4. Don't hike very early or very late in the day.
5. Make plenty of noise to signal your presence.

Encounters between bears and people in Colorado are extremely rare, but due to climatic and population pressures they have increased in the last few years. I have never seen a bear in twenty years in the state, and the likelihood of running across one is quite low. If you do encounter a bear on the trail, freeze initially and very slowly back away. Use a whistle, your voice, or anything available to alert the bear to your presence; usually it will take evasive action. Never run away, or the bear may mistake you for prey. If you spot a cub, take another route and get as far away as possible, as adult bears are highly protective of their offspring.

Do everything you can to keep your food and garbage away from bears, and away from you when camping. If your campsite has a food storage facility (in the Uncompahgre backcountry, it will not), use it. Otherwise, choose a sturdy tree branch, and hang your food and garbage at least 10 feet off the ground and at least 4 feet

◀ *Cathy Crick along the Little Elk Trail.*

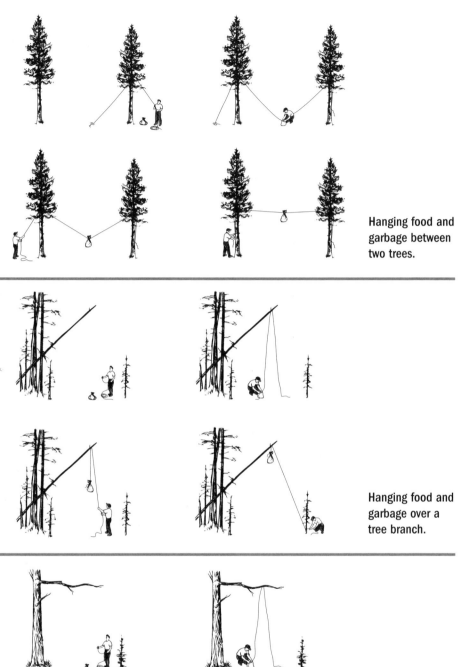

Hanging food and garbage between two trees.

Hanging food and garbage over a tree branch.

Hanging food and garbage over a leaning tree.

from the trunk. Above timberline use a cliff, boulder, or anything that's available. Store food and garbage in airtight (zipper closing, if possible) bags to contain odors. The best hanging method is to attach a rock or stick to the other end of a nylon cord and toss it over the branch to act as a counterweight. Hang anything that has an odor, including cooking gear, utensils, and garbage. Try to keep food and its odors off your clothing, and hang it as well if in doubt. For your safety, your tent or bivouac sack must be a food- and odor-free zone, so store your pack with toothpaste and other toiletries over a branch, too.

Keep meal planning and cooking simple, creating as little food odor as possible. Never cook in your tent except in a weather emergency. Wash dishes immediately after eating, and do so at least 100 yards downwind from your campsite and away from water sources. Parties should camp at least 100 yards from one another and up-wind from cooking areas. Food and other materials should be hung in the cooking area and no closer than necessary to the tent sites.

Report any bear sighting to the nearest Forest Service office at first opportunity, as the Forest Service will often attempt to manage wildlife to help prevent danger-ous situations from occurring.

Mountain Lions

Being in mountain lion country also adds a certain risk to your hike, but encounters between humans and these shy animals are even more rare than human–bear en-counters. Cougars prey largely on deer and other small animals, so if you see deer or their scat and tracks, you can assume that mountain lions also inhabit the area. Take the following five steps to help prevent dangerous encounters with mountain lions:

1. Don't hike alone (is this beginning to sound familiar?).
2. Keep children and pets in your group, with the adults.
3. Lions are most active at dawn and dusk, so be on the alert during these times.
4. Watch for signs of lion habitat and activity.
5. Know what to do in case of an encounter.

The last point, how to react if you encounter a mountain lion, deserves elabora-tion. Most cats will practice avoidance, indifference, or at worst, curiosity toward hu-mans, but you should be prepared if the encounter goes beyond this. Follow these steps if you encounter a cat:

• Recognize threatening behavior: If the cat is within 50 yards, is crouched or staring intently at you, it may be weighing the possibility of an attack. Maintain eye contact and make yourself appear as large as possible by waving your arms steadily above your head. Talk in a calm but loud voice to warn others. If your group has children or pets, pick them up without bending over (small size may help the lion mistake you for prey) and while maintaining eye contact. Give the animal an op-portunity to move on by backing away slowly.

• If you are attacked, try to remain standing, and fight back with all available re-sources! A weapon can be a rock, a tree branch, a knife, pepper spray, or any other solid object. Help defend other people in your group if necessary, but it is not recommended that you intervene to protect pets.

• If the mountain lion is more than 50 yards away and becomes aware of you, it is likely only curious and presents little risk to adults. Gather children and pets together, and move away slowly while keeping the animal in your peripheral vision. Scan the ground as you go for potential weapons to use in case the cat attacks.

• Report any encounter to the Forest Service as soon as possible. Describe the location and other details as specifically as possible. If there is an attack, leave the area without disturbing the site, as the Forest Service will need an undisturbed "crime scene" in order to best manage the situation.

Hypothermia

Exposure to inclement weather is the principal danger faced by hikers and backpackers. Even in midsummer in Colorado, and particularly during the late-July and August monsoon season, it is possible to encounter very cold and wet weather conditions. Hypothermia occurs when the body's core temperature falls below normal, reducing blood supply to the brain and other vital tissues. It is caused by a combination of cold weather, wind, and wetness, and even in extreme conditions it is preventable. By staying in camp during cold, wet weather and by carrying sufficient dry clothing of the right type, hypothermia should never become an issue for hikers.

The best measure to prevent hypothermia is to keep yourself and your clothing dry. Dress in layers made of breathable fabric, particularly for the inner layers. Use a waterproof pack cover and pack your gear with the primary goal of keeping everything dry. Whenever possible carry full-length rain gear, and carry it where it is quickly accessible. Your tent and sleeping bag may end up being your last defense against discomfort and even hypothermia, so assure the weatherproofness of your tent before your trip, and do everything possible to keep your sleeping bag dry.

The symptoms of early-stage hypothermia can be difficult to recognize, but include severe shivering, slurred speech, numbness, loss of motor control, and drowsiness. If any of these symptoms are present, it is important to ensure that the victim be made warm and dry. Change the victim to dry clothing and get him or her to dry shelter (tent and sleeping bag) immediately. Have the victim drink warm fluids and share a sleeping bag with a nonhypothermic person. In advanced to severe cases where the victim is beginning to lose consciousness, keep the victim awake at all costs.

Lightning

The high country of Colorado is one of the most thunderstorm-prone areas of the United States, and if you spend time in the mountains you must be prepared for wet conditions and lightning. Although late spring and summer are the prime season, thunderstorms can occur year-round, even during snowstorms. The pattern of occurrence is predictable, however, and there are a number of steps you can take to avoid the dangers of lightning.

The number one rule is to do as much of your hiking before noon as you can. Day after day, crystal-clear summer mornings in Colorado turn dark and violent by early afternoon, and higher elevations tend to develop dangerous conditions earlier in the day. Avoid hiking above timberline if thunderstorms are approaching or forecast, as you will have little or no protection from the elements. Thunderstorms often form directly over the higher peaks of the San Juans, and can move in any direction. Lightning can occur far in advance of the portion of the storm that produces rain. If a storm is close enough for you to hear thunder, then it is close enough to present a lightning danger!

The wilderness boundary, Dexter Creek Trail.

If a storm approaches when you are on exposed terrain, seek the lowest ground available that is not holding water. Even descending a short distance from a ridgetop greatly decreases the danger. Heavily forested areas are generally quite safe, but avoid seeking shelter under isolated trees. Stay out of shallow caves and rock overhangs, as they conduct electricity. You may get warning that a lightning strike is imminent; buzzing noises from metal equipment parts, your hair "standing on end," and an odd itchy feeling are all signs that the danger is immediate. Keep members of your party as far apart as possible. On open ground do not lie down, but rather assume a crouched position with only your feet touching the ground. Crouch on a ground pad or sleeping bag, if available, for further insulation against ground currents. In a tent crouch in your sleeping bag on top of a ground pad.

Finally, lightning exposure is only one of many reasons for at least one member of your party to be trained in the use of CPR and wilderness first aid.

Trail Etiquette

While on the trail, you may encounter other hikers and people on horseback. When hiking downhill, always yield the trail to those hiking uphill. Uphill hikers may, of course, choose to yield to the downhillers, thereby justifying a quick breather! On level ground the hiker with the lighter pack should yield. Horseback riders have the right-of-way over hikers regardless of direction; the job of the hiker is to let the animals by without startling them. Hikers should move off the trail to the downhill side, and must avoid making any noises or movements that might startle the pack animals. Speaking to the riders will help make the horses aware of and more relaxed in your presence. If on horseback, please reinforce this behavior by thanking hikers who show the proper etiquette.

Zero Impact

Nowadays most wilderness users want to walk softly, but may not be aware of how their actions affect the outdoor experiences of others. Many practices of the past, such as building water-control trenches and large campfire rings, or cutting live trees for shelter, leave durable scars on the land and are no longer acceptable.

Because wild places are becoming rare and the number of backcountry visitors is mushrooming, a new code of ethics is growing. Today we all must leave no clues that we were there. Enjoy the wild, but leave no indication of your visit.

FALCON'S ZERO-IMPACT PRINCIPLES
- Leave with everything you brought in.
- Leave no sign of your visit.
- Leave the landscape as you found it.

Most of us know better than to litter—in or out of the backcountry. Be sure you leave nothing along the trail or in your campsite. Pack out all items, no matter how small, including orange peels, flip tops, cigarette butts, and gum wrappers, and do your best to pick up any trash others leave behind.

Stay on the main trail, even when it is ankle-deep in mud. As you search out drier ground to avoid mud, the trail widens and forms "braids." For the same reason, do your best to climb or crawl directly over fallen trees; creating temporary trails around obstacles increases erosion and our impact on the forest. Within a group, hike single-file.

Don't pick up souvenirs, such as rocks, antlers, or wildflowers. The next person wants to see them, too, and collecting them violates many regulations.

Avoid making loud noises on the trail (unless you are in bear country) or in camp. Be courteous—remember, sound travels easily in the backcountry.

Carry a lightweight trowel to bury human waste 6 to 8 inches deep and at least 200 feet from any water source. Pack out used toilet paper.

Go without a campfire. Carry a stove for cooking and flashlight, candle lantern, or headlamp for light. For emergencies, learn how to build a no-trace fire.

Camp in obviously used sites when they are available. Otherwise, camp and cook on durable surfaces such as bedrock, sand, or bare ground.

Sign in at trailhead registers; this is the only way for land management agencies to accurately gauge land use.

No motorized travel is allowed in the Uncompahgre Wilderness. Parties on horseback are limited by regulation to fifteen people and animals in aggregate—for example, ten people and five pack animals. Take as few animals as possible to minimize the impact of your party, and keep them in dry areas. When stopped, tie animals to trees at least 8 inches in diameter. During overnight stops tie them to a high line between two trees, at least 200 feet from any water source and away from camp, so that they can roam. If you begin to see impacts to soil or vegetation, move the horses to a different location. Carry only certified weed-free feed.

History of the Uncompahgre Wilderness

The Uncompahgre Wilderness is located in the north-central part of the San Juan Mountains, the most remote of Colorado's many high mountain ranges. The San Juans are unique in that they cover a massive 10,000 square miles of area, and they contain thirteen peaks over 14,000 feet high and many more over 13,000 feet high. Unlike the vast majority of the highest ranges in the Rocky Mountains, they are of relatively recent volcanic origin. From approximately 70 million years to 20 million years ago, the area was subject to violent and widespread volcanic activity. Careful mapping by geologists has identified as many as thirteen centers of volcanic eruption, two of which were centered near the present-day towns of Lake City and Silverton. A variety of ash flows, breccias, conglomerates, and other volcanic rocks were deposited to become today's bedrock. The landscape has resulted from slight uplift and erosion that continues today.

Natural History

Present-day landforms and climate have resulted in a wide variety of ecosystems in the San Juan Mountains. An understanding of ecosystems can greatly enhance the experience of being in the outdoors, so in the following paragraphs I will describe those you are likely to encounter in the Uncompahgre Wilderness.

Mountain riparian ecosystems are encountered on the initial portions of many Uncompahgre hikes as you follow major stream valleys into higher ground. They are characterized by energetic mountain streams intermixed with ponds, lakes, and boggy wetland areas. Vegetation communities are extremely diverse and complex, dominated by shrubby willows and other moisture-loving species (known as phreatophytes) interspersed with grassy sandbars and groves of trees. Ponds and lakes at higher elevation tend to be deep, cold, and poor in nutrients and organic matter. Animal communities in riparian areas are also diverse, as the vegetation provides abundant food and protective cover.

The ponderosa pine–Douglas fir forest ecosystem is present in the Uncompahgre at elevations ranging up to approximately 10,000 feet, so you may see this also on the early portions of Uncompahgre hikes. The northern valleys of the Uncompahgre contain large areas of this ecosystem, as do the lower foothills areas near Lake City. The two types of forest stands frequently occur in close proximity to one another, with ponderosas occupying dry, warm sites and the Douglas fir dominating on cool, moist north slopes. Ponderosas can grow quite large in the southern Rocky Mountains. Mature ponderosas can be identified by a thick reddish bark that has a scent of vanilla. Their thick bark protects them from all but the most severe fires, and ponderosas actually thrive following ground fires that are commonly started by

Fall colors in North Henson Creek.

lightning. Although Douglas firs can reach impressive size in the mountains of the Pacific states, in the southern Rockies they are limited by cold temperatures and more arid conditions, and rarely exceed 100 feet in height. Douglas fir stands generally withstand ground fires, but are susceptible to severe crown fires. A large variety of bird species find their homes in ponderosa–Douglas fir forests. Squirrels, chipmunks, various mouse and lizard species, mule deer, and elk also frequent these forests.

Every outdoor enthusiast in Colorado is familiar with the mature aspen groves that thrive between elevations of 6,000 and 10,000 feet. At lower elevations they are often limited to small stands located in moist pockets of ground. At the middle elevations they form large stands, while near the upper limit of their elevation range they tend to occupy sunny slopes that are protected from severe winds. Groves of large aspen trees support a rich, shaded understory of grasses and forbs. Aspen trees often become established in areas disturbed by logging or fire by dispersing seeds over a very large area. Seeds can germinate only on bare soil in moist conditions, and very few do so successfully. Once seedlings are established, the trees reproduce by suckering, a process of sprouting new trees from a system of widespread, shallow, tightly connected roots. Aspen are prone to a variety of fungal diseases, and the wood is fragile and easily damaged by heavy snows and windfall. Aspen forests over time give way to Douglas and subalpine fir and Engelmann spruce, which take advantage of the shady understory and rich soils of aspen groves. Many rodent and bird species are found in aspen-covered areas, and young aspen seedlings provide important forage for elk and mule deer populations.

Engelmann spruce–subalpine fir forests run continuously through the highest forested areas of the Uncompahgre Wilderness and other areas of the central and southern Rocky Mountains, at elevations from about 9,500 to above 11,000 feet. These areas have a cool, moist climate, and the forest itself accentuates this effect by shading the floor and holding its snowpack well into summer. The spruce-fir forest is very effective in trapping and storing moisture, and it is largely the melting of heavy snowpacks at these elevations that provides water to western Colorado's towns and farms. This type of forest is susceptible to numerous health threats, including the spruce budworm (which attacks both species), the spruce beetle, various fungal diseases, high winds, and lightning. The forest is protected from frequent fire damage by the wet weather, and from logging by typically difficult terrain. After an area at high elevation is burned or otherwise disturbed, it is often colonized first by lodgepole pine and aspen, to be replaced by Engelmann spruce and subalpine fir within about fifty years. The high forests support a less diverse set of animal species than do Douglas fir, ponderosa pine, and aspen areas, though interesting species such as the snowshoe hare, the bobcat, and the Canada lynx join mice, squirrels, and a variety of bird life here. The upper transition to the alpine tundra (known as krummholz), marked by severe cold and wind conditions, is a typically narrow belt of stunted, wind-tortured varieties of the same tree species.

The alpine tundra ecosystem lies in the harsh zone above timberline, sharing many plant types with its equivalent in the Arctic. Soils are frozen for most of the year, and there is little protection from the constant cold winds. With a growing season of only about two months, the climate is too harsh to support tree life. There are, however, a remarkable variety of plants that have adapted to living in the alpine zone. Grasses, sedges, small shrubs, and brilliantly colored wildflowers cover large areas of tundra. The plant communities are actually very complex, and are arranged on a small scale that depends on the time length of snow cover in a particular spot. There are no mammal species that are limited to the alpine tundra, although many will stray onto it during the warmer summer months. Snowshoe hares, chipmunks, coyotes, bobcats, and foxes may also be seen. The white-tailed ptarmigan has evolved camouflage in the form of a white surface in winter that changes to mottled brown in summer. Marmots and pikas will be familiar to hikers who frequent the tundra, and mule deer and elk are able to find forage here as well as in the lower subalpine forests.

Human History

The earliest human history of southwestern Colorado involves a nomadic tribe of Native Americans, the Tabeguache Ute, who lived throughout central and western Colorado, northern New Mexico, and eastern Utah. The landscapes around the Rocky Mountains provided all of the food and shelter that the Utes needed to survive. In 1765 and 1776 Spanish expeditions passed through the area in search of an overland route from Santa Fe to the Pacific Ocean, and it is likely that some of the visitors did a little gold prospecting along the way. The Wheeler and Hayden surveys, sponsored by the U.S. government, passed through western Colorado in 1875 and 1876, taking extensive notes and drawing maps of the territories. When rich gold discoveries were made near Lake City in 1871 and near Ouray and Silverton beginning in 1875, European Americans came into the area in droves. Ouray and Lake City developed in almost parallel fashion during the next few years, with schools, saloons, churches, blacksmith shops, newspapers, and other forms of civilization springing up to support the needs of the prospectors.

Most of the land in the San Juan Mountains was ceded by the Utes to the visitors in 1874, and the two groups managed for some time to live a peaceful side-by-side existence. Chief Ouray was one of the architects of the land deal, and is largely credited with maintaining the peace during this time. The Meeker Massacre of 1879 was the beginning of the end, however, and after Chief Ouray died in 1880, the Utes were pushed westward into Utah. Transportation in the form of railroads and toll roads slowly improved, thanks mostly to the remarkable Otto Mears. His company developed the transportation corridors that most of today's roads and highways follow, including the "Million Dollar Highway" over Red Mountain Pass. The most prolific mines were in the areas south and southwest of Ouray, and Mears's toll roads meant that Ouray flourished economically long before Silverton did. Still, the costs of extraction, processing, and transportation of the ore were enormous, and it is likely that despite the very rich ore deposits, 90 percent of the operations never turned a profit. During this time Ridgway and Montrose developed as centers of transportation and agriculture.

Gold discoveries near Ouray in the late 1880s helped it to survive the 1893 silver crash that ruined the economy of Lake City. Gold discoveries in the latter area in the mid-1880s were short-lived, with production peaking in 1895; by the turn of the century, Lake City's population had been cut in half. From 1900 to the 1930s, precious metals prices did very little, only the best-endowed mines were able to continue operating, and the entire area slowly lost population. World War II revived the industry somewhat, but it was the 1950s before the area began to recover with an influx of tourism dollars that continues today. The long mining history in the San Juans and other parts of the Rocky Mountains left a legacy of seemingly intractable environmental issues, particularly those of erosion and degraded water quality. More recently, however, technology and reclamation laws and practices have combined to help reduce the environmental impacts of mining.

As early as 1930 portions of today's Uncompahgre Wilderness and the surrounding national forest were protected from development by inclusion in the designated Uncompahgre Primitive Area. The Big Blue Wilderness (with nearly identical boundaries to those of the Uncompahgre of today) was established by the 1980 Colorado Wilderness Act, and the name was changed to the Uncompahgre Wilderness by the Colorado Wilderness Act of 1993.

How to Use This Book

There is a tremendous variety of hiking choices in the Uncompahgre Wilderness, from relatively easy day hikes to multiday, very strenuous backpacking outings and peak climbs. You can easily adapt any of the described hikes to your needs. For example, you can make an easy day hike out of the first 3 miles of a trail that is described as a difficult, multiple-day backpacking outing (examples are given in certain individual trail descriptions). Similarly, loop hikes beginning and ending at a trailhead can often be created from two or more hikes described in this book. There is also ample opportunity for destination hikes that cross the area to a different trailhead, assuming that you can arrange for a two-vehicle shuttle or a ride to or from one of the trailheads. This book describes in detail several examples of each type of hike, but with some imagination the possibilities are endless. By sampling the hikes described in this book, you will learn your way around the Uncompahgre, after which you can compose your own day hikes and backpacking adventures.

Each trail description in this book begins with a brief summary of the hike and the **Type of Hike.** These two descriptors will help you narrow your choices if your time is limited. The approximate **Distance** involved in a given hike is listed next. Please note that these are estimated distances; most have not been measured with a distance wheel, and any means of measurement will have something less than 100 percent accuracy. A one-word summary of relative **Difficulty** is also given in each trail description. Any additional considerations that should be taken into account are included under the heading **Trail conditions.** These may include tricky or dangerous creek crossings, frequent wet or muddy sections of trail, long distances above timberline with exposure to lightning and the elements, heavy trail use, or anything else of which hikers should be aware. The Trail Conditions section also points out trails that require map-and-compass and route-finding skills. **Maps** provides a list of the U.S. Geological Survey 7.5-minute quadrangles that will be of use on the hike. Finally, **Management** lists the Forest Service district or districts to be contacted for more information.

The Trail Finder in the Appendix lists the hikes in order from Easy to Difficult. Please remember that these difficulty designations are only my own opinion, and that your own conditioning, weather and snowmelt conditions, and many other factors will contribute to the difficulty of a hike. In addition, the terms are intended to be relative only to the Uncompahgre Wilderness; an Easy hike here may be more strenuous than an Easy hike in other terrain. Easy trails are those that can be hiked in approximately a half day by someone in good physical condition, are no more than about 6 or 7 miles in length, and are characterized by easy to moderate gradients. Moderate trails are longer or more strenuous, and will require most of a day of hiking to complete. Difficult trails combine distance and gradient such that good conditioning is essential.

Each trail description is accompanied by a shaded relief map. For shorter day hikes, the maps in this book may be sufficient for finding and staying on the trail. It is highly recommended, however, that you carry and use the appropriate USGS maps for your hike.

Since the initial prerequisite to completing any hike is to successfully locate the trailhead, the heading for each hike is followed by a section titled **Finding the trailhead.** This gives a description of the vehicle approach to the trailhead. Most mileages were measured directly with a vehicle odometer; however, consider these mileages to be approximate. Finding the Trailhead will also describe whether anything other than a typical passenger car is required to reach the trailhead. The availability of camping and sanitary facilities in the area of the trailhead is also discussed in this section.

A section titled **Options** may be provided at the end of hike descriptions. These will list extended hike or side hike possibilities that may be pursued in conjunction with a given hike.

All hike descriptions include a listing of **Landmarks** such as trail junctions, lakes, stream crossings, and other prominent features, with approximate mileages from the trailhead. These are intended to help you stay on course and measure progress.

Although each of the trails has been given a name by the USDA Forest Service, many have also been assigned a number. Since the trail numbers are sometimes used on trail signs and markers, they are also given in the headers and trail descriptions. There is not, however, a simple one-to-one correspondence between described hikes and named trails; rather, this book describes actual day hikes and overnight backpacks that you can expect to find particularly enjoyable. Certain sections of trail that combine logically with others may be described more than once, while at least one section of trail (the very north end of the Ridge Stock Driveway) is not described in this book.

Ten of the hikes listed in this book have a mountain summit as a destination. They have been chosen because they are hiking peaks and can be ascended without encountering any technical climbing or exposed scrambling (Wetterhorn Peak is an exception, but is included because it is a "fourteener" and a very prominent summit in this part of the San Juans). Peaks such as Precipice Peak, Dunsinane Mountain, and Point 13,411 (this has been referred to elsewhere as the Heisshorn) have not been described in this book because they involve either considerable exposure or route-finding difficulties, or both. Brief descriptions of routes up these mountains are found in Robert Ormes's classic work, *Guide to the Colorado Mountains.*

Day Hikes

1 Bear Creek National Recreation Trail to Yellowjacket Mine

Forest Service Trail 241

A diverse hike up a spectacular canyon to a scenic mine site.

Type of hike: Day hike. This trail enters the southwestern corner of the Uncompahgre Wilderness, with numerous options available for extended backpacking trips.

Distance: 7.2 miles out-and-back (Yellowjacket Mine).

13.5 miles (American Flats loop).

Difficulty: Easy (Yellowjacket Mine).

Difficult (American Flats loop).

Trail conditions: The Bear Creek National Recreation Trail is quite easy to follow for its entire length. A few sections have eroded to a narrow shelf, but should present no danger to the surefooted hiker. There are vertigo-inducing drops in places; be particularly careful carrying a heavy pack. This is a relatively high-traffic trail as far as the Yellowjacket Mine. Campsites and water are easily found starting at about 2.5 miles and in the area near the mine.

Maps: USGS Ouray, Ironton, Handies Peak, and Wetterhorn Peak 7.5-minute quadrangles.

Management: Ouray Ranger District, Uncompahgre National Forest.

Finding the trailhead: From the southernmost intersection on the main street of Ouray, drive south on U.S. Highway 550 for 2.3 miles to the trailhead, located just south of a highway tunnel. Parking is available on both sides of the road. No sanitary facilities are present at the trailhead, and there is no space available for camping. Nearby campsites are located at the U.S. Forest Service Amphitheater Campground, just south of Ouray, and informal sites can be found 6 to 8 miles farther south on U.S. 550.

Landmarks

0.0 Bear Creek National Recreation Trailhead.

2.5 Tributary crossing.

3.6 Yellowjacket Mine; turnaround for shorter hike.

(4.0) Junction with trail from Engineer Pass.

(5.7) Saddle leading to American Flats.

(7.5) Engineer Pass.

(9.5) Junction with Bear Creek National Recreation Trail; turn left (west).

7.2 (13.5) Bear Creek National Recreation Trailhead.

The Hike

Almost all of the Bear Creek National Recreation Trail (including the entire day hike described here) is located outside the boundaries of the Uncompahgre Wilderness, but if extended into American Flats the Bear Creek provides a spectacular entry into the southwest portion of the wilderness area. It is a wonderfully diverse trail, from

Bear Creek National Recreation Trail to Yellowjacket Mine

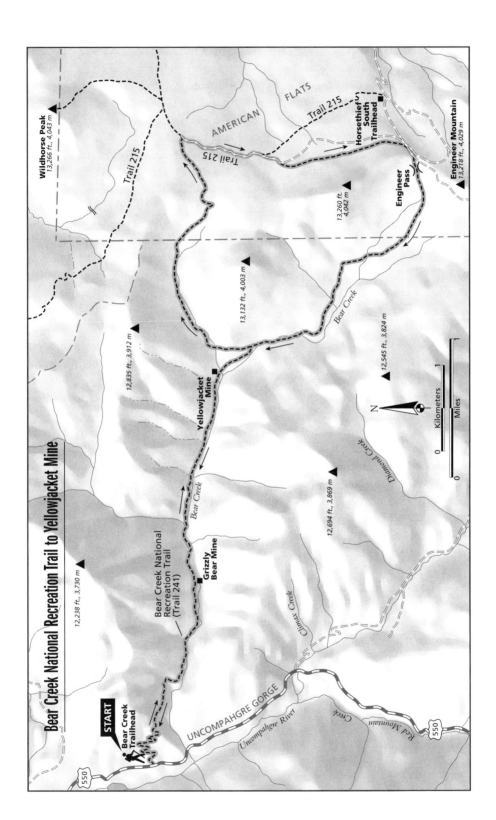

Wildhorse Peak
13,266 ft., 4,043 m

Trail 215

AMERICAN FLATS

Trail 215

Trail 215

Horsethief South Trailhead

Engineer Mountain
13,218 ft., 4,029 m

13,260 ft.,
4,042 m

Engineer Pass

13,132 ft., 4,003 m

Bear Creek

12,835 ft., 3,912 m

Yellowjacket Mine

12,545 ft., 3,824 m

N

Kilometers

Miles

0

0

12,238 ft., 3,730 m

Bear Creek National Recreation Trail (Trail 241)

Bear Creek

Grizzly Bear Mine

12,694 ft., 3,869 m

Diamond Creek

Climax Creek

START

Bear Creek Trailhead

550

UNCOMPAHGRE GORGE

Uncompahgre River

Red Mountain Creek

550

rocky switchbacks and narrow cliff-bound shelves to waterfalls and finally to high-alpine tundra. The Bear Creek Trail is sure to satisfy, either as a day hike or as an approach to a longer hike in the heart of the Uncompahgre.

The trailhead is located just south of the tunnel, on the west side of U.S. 550, 2.3 miles south of Ouray. As the trail leaves the highway, it crosses above the tunnel and tackles the very steep, cliff-strewn mountainside above. Numerous switchbacks armored with slate bedrock enable the hiker to gain elevation quickly, and in fifteen minutes or so the highway noise is reduced to a distant rumble. The last switchback is located at the base of a steep cliff of volcanic rock. Cross the top of the slate scree slope and continue across a ledge heading uphill and south. As the trail begins to turn the corner into the drainage of Bear Creek at about 0.9 mile, Red Mountain to the south and the Sneffels Range to the west come progressively into view.

The next half mile is fairly level and passes under several 300-foot cliffs. These portions of the trail are potentially subject to rockfall, particularly in wet or windy weather, so move quickly and carry a heightened level of awareness through these sections. An interesting geological attraction is the exposures of the famous "giant ripples" of Ignacio Quartzite; these can be seen in a couple of places on the north-facing cliffs across Bear Creek. For another half mile the trail follows ledges 200 feet or so above the creek, with some very steep drops below. Drop down and right across a tributary drainage at approximately 2.5 miles from the trailhead. About 500 feet upstream on this tributary is a waterfall that makes a good destination for a relatively easy 5-mile day hike.

To continue toward the Yellowjacket Mine, proceed from the tributary crossing east toward Bear Creek, where pleasant campsites with water are available (remember to follow trail and water camping buffer guidelines). Follow steeper grades on a very pleasant trail along the north side of Bear Creek. The remains of the Yellow-jacket Mine are reached near timberline, at about 3.6 miles; water supplies are abundant in the area of the mine. Enjoy a lunch and the timberline view here before retracing your steps to the trailhead.

For very fit hikers or for those equipped to spend a night out, the following paragraphs describe a fine extension of this hike into American Flats and to Engineer Pass. The extension hike is described in a clockwise direction, as this will expose you to the noise of four-wheelers at Engineer Pass for a slightly shorter period of time. Glance at the western portion of the Trails Illustrated map "Silverton, Ouray, Telluride, Lake City" and you will easily spot this compelling hike.

From the Yellowjacket Mine hike south-southeast on a well-marked trail into the southern of the two drainages that come together in the area of the mine. In only a few minutes, you will reach a trail junction with a sign indicating the direction and distance back to U.S. 550. From the junction take a trail heading north and northeast

Giant ripples along the Bear Creek Trail. ▶

up a steady grade. Follow this to an easy stream crossing. On the north side of the creek, follow what appears to be an old roadbed for about 0.3 mile into the upper basin above tree line. If you lose the trail, try to trend northeast, then east, without losing elevation, until the trail becomes obvious again. Continue generally east through the wildflower-filled tundra basin toward the obvious low point (also the wilderness area boundary) on the ridge ahead. From the high saddle, follow switchbacks on a good trail downhill into American Flats. This remarkable area presents fine views of the Uncompahgre's high peaks to the northeast, and provides access to the remainder of the wilderness area via the Ridge Stock Driveway (Trail 233; see Hike 32).

Once on level ground in American Flats, turn to the south along the eastern base of the ridge (there is no obvious track to follow at first). After a few hundred yards, try to pick up a faint roadbed that narrows to a trail and leads south-southwest to Engineer Pass. Assuming the usual assortment of two-wheel and four-wheel vehicles hanging around and moving over the pass, you will want to quickly find the trail that descends from the pass to the west-southwest. Do not take the higher shelf trail toward the northwest; it dead-ends high on the ridge. The descending trail soon takes up a northwesterly course through the upper Bear Creek basin, crossing the creek once up high and twice more near timberline. At approximately 2 miles below Engineer Pass, you will encounter the familiar signed trail junction, indicating that 4 miles down the canyon, past the Yellowjacket Mine, will return you to U.S. 550.

Options

From American Flats there are many choices to extend the hike. You can descend back to U.S. 550 north of Ouray via the Horsethief Trail (Trail 215, Hike 27), a vigorous and spectacular 15-mile hike requiring a car shuttle. A second option continues east from the base of the ridge in American Flats. This places the hiker on the Ridge Stock Driveway (Trail 233, Hike 32), which leads northeast into the central area of the Uncompahgre Wilderness. From the Ridge Stock Driveway, connections can be made to many of the trails leading to the north and south sides of the wilderness area.

2 Horsethief Trail to Bridge of Heaven

Forest Service Trail 215

The Bridge of Heaven is an exposed, scenic ridge with views of Grand Mesa, the West Elk Mountains, and the surrounding peaks.

Type of hike: Day hike.
Distance: 10.8 miles out-and-back.
Difficulty: Moderate.
Trail conditions: The trail is well maintained for its entire length. There is no water available between the trailhead and Bridge of Heaven.

Maps: USGS Ouray and Wetterhorn Peak 7.5-minute quadrangles.
Management: Ouray Ranger District, Uncompahgre National Forest.

Finding the trailhead: From the Hot Springs pool near the north end of Ouray, drive north on U.S. Highway 550 for 1.6 miles. Turn right and drive up the Dexter Creek Road (Forest Road 871/County Road 14). Stay on the main road for a total of 2.5 miles to a switchback and bridge. Trail mileages are given with this as the starting point, and passenger cars may want to park here. Continue for another 1.2 miles on foot or in your high-clearance vehicle to the Wedge Mine and the well-marked trailhead. Camping is possible at both the Dexter Creek and Horsethief Trailheads, but flat space is scarce and there are no sanitary facilities.

Landmarks

0.0 Dexter Creek Trailhead. Parking for passenger cars without high clearance.
1.2 Wedge Mine.
1.3 Horsethief Trailhead.
2.9 Clearing with view of Lake Lenore and Ridgway.
3.1 Top of ridge.
5.4 Bridge of Heaven; turnaround.
10.8 Dexter Creek Trailhead.

The Hike

The hike to Bridge of Heaven is a favorite of locals in the Uncompahgre Valley, and deservedly so. A well-worn trail, wide variety of terrain and vegetation, fine vantage points, generally moderate difficulty, and a spectacular destination add up to a wonderful hiking experience. If you are parking at the Dexter Creek Trailhead, follow the road across the creek and uphill to the west. Stay on the main road, although one short diversion to the west at a switchback is worthwhile for its view of Whitehouse Mountain, across the Uncompahgre Valley to the west. After 1.2 miles the remains of the Wedge Mine appear on the left, and the well-marked Horsethief Trailhead is a few hundred yards farther along.

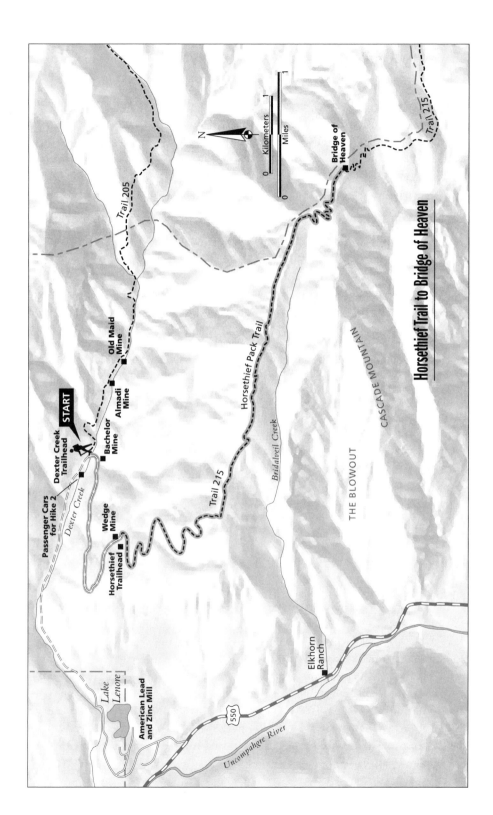

Horsethief Trail to Bridge of Heaven

N

Kilometers

1

0

Miles

1

0

Trail 205

Trail 215

Bridge of Heaven

Horsethief Pack Trail

Old Maid Mine

Almadi Mine

Bachelor Mine

Dexter Creek Trailhead

START

Passenger Cars for Hike 2

Dexter Creek

Wedge Mine

Horsethief Trailhead

Trail 215

Bridalveil Creek

THE BLOWOUT

CASCADE MOUNTAIN

Lake Lenore

American Lead and Zinc Mill

Elkhorn Ranch

550

Uncompahgre River

After signing in at the trailhead, begin hiking uphill in a mixed spruce-aspen forest. The first 1.5 miles of the trail climbs the north-facing hillside via many switchbacks, in the process wandering more than is shown on the USGS Ouray quadrangle map. The trail has been realigned in several places to reduce the steepness of the climb, but it is easy enough to stay on the correct footway. A fine view west toward Whitehouse Mountain opens up at one point, but most of the hiking is under tree cover. At just under 3 miles (about 1.6 miles from the Horsethief Trailhead), enter a clearing overlooking Lake Lenore, Ridgway, and the Uncompahgre River Valley to the northwest. At the top of the clearing, meet a ridgeline at 3.1 miles (1.8 miles from the trailhead) with a sign indicating another 2.3 miles to Bridge of Heaven. If an easy half-day hike is sufficient to satisfy you, this saddle is a worthy destination, as it gives a fine view over Ouray to Red Mountain Pass and the Million-Dollar Highway to the south and the Camp Bird area to the southwest. Note that the trail shown on the USGS Ouray quadrangle that descends into Ouray from near this saddle no longer exists, and that the terrain below is very steep and complicated.

From the saddle the way to Bridge of Heaven is abundantly clear, toward the high point visible to the southeast. For the next mile the trail more or less follows

Dan Hippe on the pass above Difficulty Creek.

the ridgeline between the Blowout to the south and the Dexter Creek drainage to the north, ducking first around its north side to avoid some rock outcrops, then to its sunny south side. The grade is moderate but steady and tiring nonetheless. A flatter wooded area about 1.3 miles above the saddle provides a brief respite before the uphill march resumes. A northward view all the way to Grand Mesa opens up along here, and a brief clearing at about 11,450 feet reveals Dunsinane and Courthouse Mountains to the northeast. On this ridge the trail is just outside the wilderness boundary, which lies a short distance downhill toward Dexter Creek.

Leave the trees for the last time at just above 11,800 feet, and begin a series of switchbacks up an open mountainside with a fine seasonal display of wildflowers. At the fifth switchback the trail touches the ridge of Cascade Mountain rising out of Ouray, giving a glimpse over the Ouray Amphitheater. A few minutes above is the Bridge of Heaven, the destination of this hike. The view takes in Grand Mesa and the West Elk Mountains in the distance to the north and northeast, Dunsinane Mountain, Precipice Peak, Redcliff, and Coxcomb to the northeast, Red Mountains No. 1 and 2 to the south, and to the west the Sneffels Range, whose high point—Mount Sneffels—is a remarkably indistinct peak when viewed from this angle.

Options

The hike can be extended by traversing across the Difficulty Creek and Wildhorse Creek drainages to American Flats (9 miles) and the Engineer Pass Road (10 miles) on the southwestern side of the Uncompahgre. This extended hike requires a major effort involving substantial uphill sections and a lengthy car shuttle, and is most often completed in the opposite direction.

3 Dexter Creek Trail

Forest Service Trail 205

A pleasant hike over moderate terrain featuring stately aspen groves.

Type of hike: Day hike.
Distance: Up to 7.2 miles out-and-back.
Difficulty: Moderate.
Trail conditions: Short sections on the lower part of the trail are eroding. Water is available on the lower 2.8 miles of the hike. Good campsites are scarce until the ridge is reached, but there is no water available up high. The trail is easy to follow except in the early season, when it may be obscured by snowbanks and fallen timber.
Maps: USGS Ouray and Wetterhorn Peak 7.5-minute quadrangles.
Management: Ouray Ranger District, Uncompahgre National Forest.

Finding the trailhead: From the Hot Springs pool near the north end of Ouray, drive north on U.S. Highway 550 for 1.6 miles. Turn right and drive up the Dexter Creek Road (Forest Road 871/Country Road 14) for 2.5 miles to the well-marked trailhead, where the road switchbacks right, across the creek. The trailhead is easily reached by passenger cars. Although camping is possible at the trailhead, it is a mediocre site and is not recommended. Water is available at the trailhead and throughout the lower portions of this trail.

Landmarks

0.0 Dexter Creek Trailhead and Bachelor Mine remains.

0.5 Almadi Mine remains.

0.7 Old Maid Mine remains.

1.4 Wilderness boundary.

2.8 Switchback away from creek.

3.6 Top of ridgeline.

7.2 Dexter Creek Trailhead.

The Hike

The Dexter Creek Trail allows the hiker to penetrate the edge of the Uncompahgre Wilderness, but remains relatively close to civilization throughout its length. From the trailhead described above, start up the north bank of Dexter Creek, and after a short distance head north up a usually dry tributary drainage. Cross the tributary at some cairns and hike back south toward Dexter Creek. Pass the remains of the Almadi and Old Maid Mine sites, both within the first three-quarters of a mile. About ten minutes of uphill hiking past the mines leads to a saddle with a view of Point 12,714

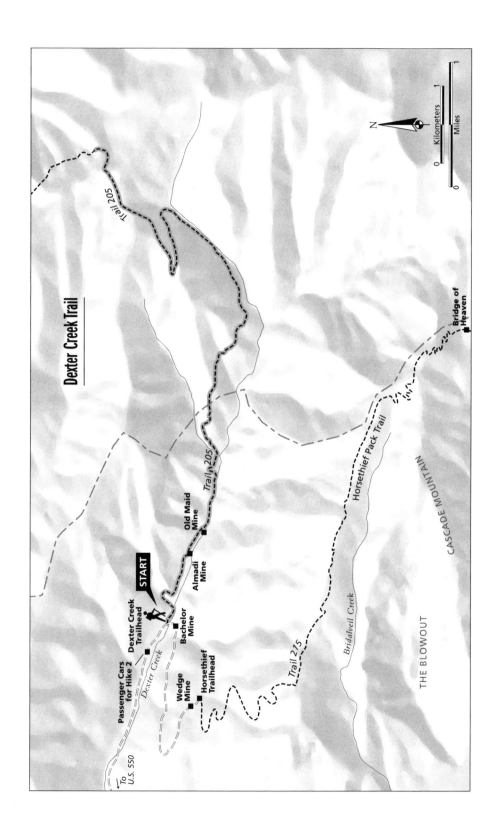

Dexter Creek Trail

Trail 205

START

Dexter Creek Trailhead

Old Maid Mine

Almadi Mine

Bachelor Mine

Wedge Mine

Horsethief Trailhead

Passenger Cars for Hike 2

Dexter Creek

To U.S. 550

Trail 205

Trail 275

Bridalveil Creek

Horsethief Pack Trail

Bridge of Heaven

CASCADE MOUNTAIN

THE BLOWOUT

N

Kilometers

Miles

1

1

0

0

to the southeast. After a brief downhill stretch and another side drainage, climb more steeply to the wilderness boundary sign at about 1.4 miles.

From the wilderness boundary another 250 feet of elevation is gained before the trail begins to level off in an open hillside of grass, oak brush, and aspen. Continue on contour with some mild uphill stretches as both the creek and trail begin to turn to the northeast. Cross beautiful aspen groves to where the creek rises to meet the trail at a distance of approximately 2 miles. The trail may be obscured by fallen timber and early-season snow for the next quarter mile or so, but it sticks closely to the streambed on the west side. Beyond a large avalanche chute on the right, begin looking for a prominent switchback uphill and to the left. Fill all water containers at this point, if necessary, as there is no further reliable supply. After the switchback, the trail soon turns back to the north-northeast in a clearing and reenters the forest; it may be obscured by fallen timber. If you lose the trail, fear not; simply keep on a course slightly east of north until you meet the ridgeline. Here the trail is better, and in

Scenery along the Dexter Creek Trail.

short order you'll reach a sign indicating the distance back to the trailhead. For an in-and-out day hike, this is the recommended destination.

Options

If you wish to complete a loop hike, the trail and ridgetop continue to the north and northwest around the top of the Cutler Creek drainage to pass over Point 11,404 and connect up with the Cutler Creek Trail. At least two options for extending the hike are possible. The first continues to the northwest (and steeply downhill) from Point 11,404 for 0.4 mile to a trail junction that is rather hard to spot, but is marked by a faint track leading downhill to the west-southwest. From here the Cutler Creek Trail (Trail 217) leads downhill 2.8 miles to the Thistle Park Trailhead. The right fork (Trail 216) can be followed northwest for an additional 5 miles to Baldy Peak. Campsites are plentiful along this ridgetop but water is not, so plan on carrying all that you'll need for the extended hikes. The connecting trails are described in more detail under Cutler Creek Loop (Hike 4), Storm Gulch to Baldy Peak (Hike 5), and Baldy Trail to Baldy Peak (Hike 6). Each of these options ends in the general vicinity of Thistle Park and the Cutler Creek Trailhead, only a few miles by car from the Dexter Creek Trailhead.

4 Cutler Creek Loop
Forest Service Trails 217 and 217.2A

A good early-season hike with views of Wetterhorn Peak and the Sneffels Range.

Type of hike: Day hike.

Distance: 6.5 mile loop.

Difficulty: Moderate.

Trail conditions: Generally dry and easy to follow, with some downed timber. Informal trailhead camping is available at Thistle Park. Water is available only in the first mile or so of the trail. This loop is described in a counter-clockwise direction, because the descent from Baldy Ridge on Trail 217.2A is the easier descent to locate.

Maps: USGS Ouray and Wetterhorn Peak 7.5-minute quadrangles. Only a very short section of trail near the high point is located on the Wetterhorn Peak quadrangle.

Management: Ouray Ranger District, Uncompahgre National Forest.

Finding the trailhead: Find the Dexter Creek Road (Forest Road 871/Country Road 14) from U.S. Highway 550, 1.6 miles north of the Ouray Hot Springs pool. Follow this road around Lake Lenore for 1 mile to a left turn marked CUTLER CREEK ROAD; this is FR 872. It crosses a bridge immediately, then proceeds north along a barren hillside. Follow the road (a bit rough and narrow but passable for passenger cars) for a total of 2.5 miles to a meadow known as Thistle Park. There are two trailheads, one at the eastern end of Thistle Park, the other where a rough road that forks left at Thistle Park crosses Cutler Creek. The Thistle Park Trailhead is described here.

Landmarks

0.0 Thistle Park Trailhead.

0.2 Wilderness boundary.

1.0 Trail 217/217.2A junction; turn right (south).

1.6 Enter large clearing.

2.8 Junction with ridgetop trail.

3.9 Left (west) onto Trail 217.2A.

5.5 Trail 217/217.2A junction; turn left (west).

6.5 Thistle Park Trailhead.

The Hike

Begin the hiking at the upper (east) end of Thistle Park, and proceed up the south side of Cutler Creek to an easy stream crossing a short distance from the trailhead. Several hundred feet of hiking on the north side of the creek leads to the wilderness boundary. Once within the wilderness, the trail gains elevation only slightly through about a half mile of alternating open meadows and forested areas. Pass a grassy knoll,

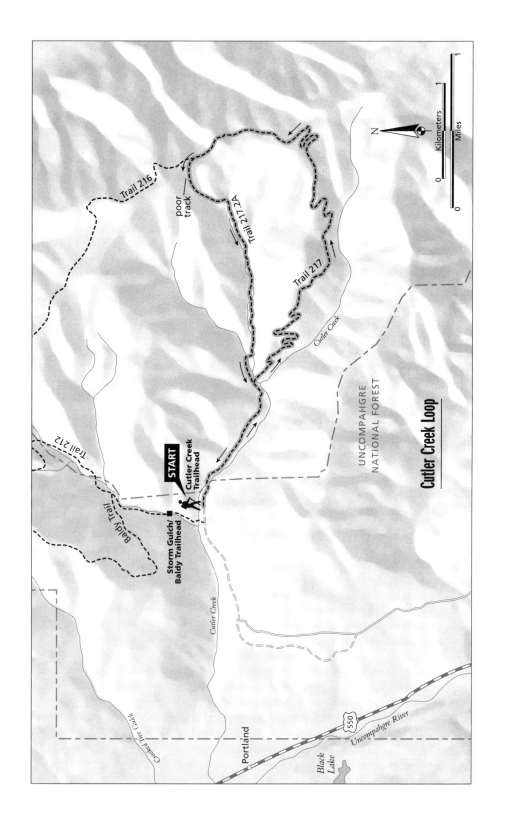

Trail 216

poor track

Trail 217.2A

Trail 217

Cutler Creek

Trail 212

Baldy Trail

START

Cutler Creek Trailhead

Storm Gulch/ Baldy Trailhead

UNCOMPAHGRE NATIONAL FOREST

Cutler Creek

Crooked Tree Gulch

Portland

550

Uncompahgre River

Black Lake

Cutler Creek Loop

N

0   1
Kilometers

0   1
Miles

The Sneffels Range viewed from the Cutler Creek Trail.

then a short flat stretch leading to a trail junction marked with a post at 1.0 mile. Trail 217.2A forks left here, while Trail 217 heads right.

Take the right-hand option (Trail 217) as it crosses a small tributary drainage and switchbacks out the south side. Turn a corner to the southeast, and make a rising traverse on the north side of Cutler Creek. After about a quarter mile of traversing, a series of switchbacks leads higher onto the south-facing slopes. Note that the trail does not attack the climb as directly as shown on the Trails Illustrated map, but rather gains elevation gradually through the use of numerous switchbacks. The grade is mild to moderate, the trail pleasant and obvious, with interspersed sunny stretches and tree cover. Eventually enter the large clearing, which is visible on the USGS Ouray quadrangle map at an elevation of approximately 9,700 feet.

Cross the clearing to the east and southeast, staying nearly on contour. The trail enters aspen on the east end of the clearing, climbs through a pair of switchbacks, then enters a higher and more easterly clearing. A rising traverse crosses the clearing about 100 vertical feet below the trees at its top. Several more switchbacks and a long traverse to the northwest finally lead to a ridgetop that rises to the east, eventually to merge with Baldy Ridge. The trail initially heads straight east up the ridgetop, but soon drops just below it to the south. More traversing, generally to the east, and a few more switchbacks bring the top of Baldy Ridge finally into view. After a substantial bit of additional climbing, meet the ridgetop trail at a small clearing and head north-northwest toward a larger clearing to descend to Trail 217.2A.

From the top of the ridge, it is also an option to simply retrace your steps down Trail 217, as Trail 217.2A is a much steeper descent. If you instead wish to complete the loop, pick up a descending trail on the northeast side of the higher, larger clearing. Follow it steeply downhill to the north-northeast, staying on or near the ridgetop, to where it begins to level off. Continue to the north and north-northwest through some smaller clearings, another mild descent, and a pleasant aspen grove. After this point keep an eye out for a trail (217.2A) that leaves the ridgetop, downhill and toward the southwest. The sign marking this trail junction was recently down on the ground and easy to miss. If you miss this trail, your best option may be to reascend to the high point and reverse Trail 217 back to the trailhead.

On Trail 217.2A descend steeply for a half mile to a clearing where the trail briefly disappears; pick it up again at the edge of the trees near the low point of the clearing. The trail is fairly obvious from here as it follows the south side of a tributary of Cutler Creek. Not far above the lower trail junction, a little more than 1 mile above the trailhead, is a switchback. Below this you will cross a small tributary several times, and in two places you will actually follow the channel for short distances. Eventually emerge onto the north bank of the channel and descend a few moderate grades to the now familiar trail junction about 1 mile from the Cutler Creek Trailhead.

Options

The Cutler Creek Loop can be combined with the Storm Gulch to Baldy Peak (Hike 5) or Baldy Trail to Baldy Peak (Hike 6) Trails to create a loop hike. Each of these options ends in the general vicinity of the Cutler Creek Trailhead. It can also be combined with the Dexter Creek Trail (Hike 3), which leads to a trailhead located only a few miles away by road (car shuttle required).

5 Storm Gulch to Baldy Peak

Forest Service Trails 212 and 216.1A

A good early-season hike with fine views of the Sneffels Range from the Baldy Trail.

Type of hike: Day hike.

Distance: 6.8-mile loop.

Difficulty: Easy.

Trail conditions: The Storm Gulch Trail has two minor stream crossings, with no water available above the second. Portions may be muddy or snow-covered, particularly early in the season. Good campsites are scarce until Baldy Ridge, where there are no water sources.

Maps: USGS Ouray 7.5-minute quadrangle.

Management: Ouray Ranger District, Uncompahgre National Forest.

Finding the trailhead: Locate the Dexter Creek Road (Forest Road 871/Country Road 14) from U.S. Highway 550, 1.6 miles north of the Ouray Hot Springs pool. Follow this road around Lake Lenore for 1.0 mile to a left turn marked CUTLER CREEK ROAD; this is FR 872. It crosses a bridge immediately, then proceeds north along a barren hillside. Follow FR 872 for a total of 2.5 miles to a meadow known as Thistle Park. Passenger cars should park here. Hike (or drive a high-clearance vehicle) 0.2 mile down a short road that leads north (left) from Thistle Park, across Cutler Creek and Storm Gulch, to the well-marked trailhead. The possibilities for trailhead camping are excellent, but there are no sanitary facilities.

Landmarks

0.0 Storm Gulch/Baldy Trailhead.

0.1 Junction with Baldy Trail; continue straight (right).

0.3 Wilderness boundary and stream crossing.

2.3 Intersect ridgetop trail (Trail 216); turn left.

3.0 Intersect Baldy Trail; continue straight on trail 216.1A.

3.5 Baldy Peak summit.

4.0 Baldy Trail; turn right.

6.7 Storm Gulch Trail junction; turn right.

6.8 Storm Gulch/Baldy Trailhead.

The Hike

The Storm Gulch Trail provides a seldom-traveled approach to the summit of Baldy Peak, and also stands on its own as an enjoyable, half-day–or–less day hike. With its relatively low elevation, Storm Gulch is suitable for early- and late-season hiking.

From the trailhead it is a short distance up Storm Gulch to where the Storm Gulch and Baldy Trails split; continue straight on the Storm Gulch Trail. Follow the

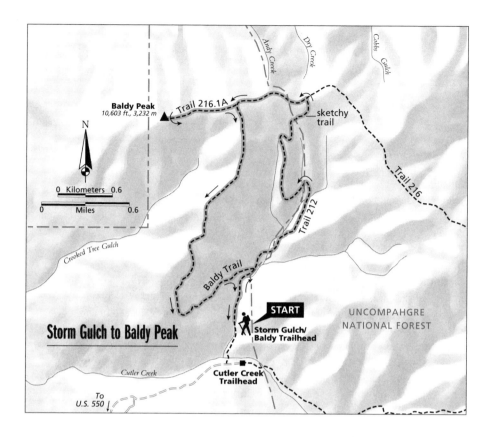

Storm Gulch to Baldy Peak

Baldy Peak
10,603 ft., 3,232 m

Trail 216.1A

sketchy trail

Trail 216

N

0 Kilometers 0.6

0 Miles 0.6

Crooked Tree Gulch

Andy Creek

Dry Creek

Cobbs Gulch

Trail 212

Baldy Trail

START

Storm Gulch/
Baldy Trailhead

UNCOMPAHGRE
NATIONAL FOREST

Cutler Creek

Cutler Creek
Trailhead

To
U.S. 550

west side of Storm Gulch for about 0.2 mile to the signed wilderness boundary and a stream crossing. Cross a meadow (the trail may be grown over by grass here) to the east and uphill for about 100 yards, then pick up the trail heading north as it climbs steeply into the trees. The trail soon levels off about 200 feet above the creek. At an elevation of approximately 9,300 feet, the creek rises to meet the trail, which crosses over and climbs a switchback up the west bank. Continue around the west side of some rock outcrops, then continue upward through denser forest of pine and aspen to the ridgetop and intersection of Trail 216.

You could of course retrace your steps down Storm Gulch at this point, but many will wish to continue the loop toward Baldy Peak. Hike to the northwest, then west along the ridgetop (Trail 216). Spectacular views of the Cimarron Divide and Sneffels Range are available from various points on the ridge. After a little more than a half mile on the ridgetop, a prominent ridge descends to the south-southwest; this is the Baldy Trail and will later be your route of descent. To complete this hike, continue west on Trail 216.1A (if the trail is not obvious, just stay near the south edge of the trees) toward the modest summit of Baldy Peak. The view from Baldy takes in the West Elk Mountains to the north and the La Sal Mountains of Utah to the west, but dominant is the rugged Sneffels Range to the southwest. Retrace your steps to the prominent ridge described earlier in this paragraph.

The Baldy Peak Trail gently descends the ridge for a little more than a mile then drops off the east side, contouring most of the way. The lower mile of the trail consists of mild switchbacks in a hillside of oak brush. You will quickly find yourself back at the junction with the Storm Gulch Trail, just minutes from the trailhead.

Options

The ridgetop trail (Trail 216) that connects Baldy and Storm Gulch can be followed southeast for approximately 3 miles to connect with the Cutler Creek Trail (Trail 217 or 217.2A, Hike 4), creating a loop hike of approximately 8 miles. Trail 216 also connects with the Dexter Creek Trail (loop distance approximately 11 miles; car shuttle required) farther to the southeast. Considerable route-finding skills may be needed to successfully complete these extended hikes, and there is no water available for a long distance.

The view south toward the Bridge of Heaven from Baldy Ridge.

6 Baldy Trail to Baldy Peak
Forest Service Trail 216.1A

A good early- or late-season hike with fine views of the Sneffels Range.

Type of hike: Day hike or short overnight.
Distance: 6.8 miles out-and-back.
Difficulty: Easy.
Trail conditions: The Baldy Trail is generally dry, sunny, and easy to follow for its entire length; no water is available except near the trailhead. Campsites are scarce until Baldy Ridge, where there are no sources of water.
Maps: USGS Ouray 7.5-minute quadrangle.
Management: Ouray Ranger District, Uncompahgre National Forest.

Finding the trailhead: Find the Dexter Creek Road (Forest Road 871) from U.S. Highway 550, 1.6 miles north of the Ouray Hot Springs pool. Follow this road around Lake Lenore for 1.0 mile to a left turn marked CUTLER CREEK ROAD; this is FR 872. It crosses a bridge immediately, then proceeds north along a barren hillside. Follow FR 872 for a total of 2.5 miles to a meadow known as Thistle Park. Passenger cars should park here. Hike (or drive a high-clearance vehicle) 0.2 mile down a short road that leads north (left) from Thistle Park, across Cutler Creek and Storm Gulch, to the well-marked trailhead. Informal camping is available in Thistle Park and at the trailhead, but there are no sanitary facilities.

Landmarks

0.0 Storm Gulch/Baldy Trailhead.
0.1 Junction with Baldy Trail; turn left.
1.8 Saddle on ridge.
3.0 Intersect ridgetop trail (Trail 216); turn left onto trail 216.1A.
3.5 Baldy Peak summit.
6.8 Storm Gulch/Baldy Trailhead.

The Hike

The Baldy and Storm Gulch Trails are among the best day hikes in the Uncompahgre Wilderness, combining easy to moderate grades, fine views of the surrounding mountains, and easy access by passenger cars. The Baldy Trail is by far the more popular route to Baldy Peak, as it is slightly shorter and sunnier than its neighbor Storm Gulch. Because of the relatively low elevation and sunny southeastern aspect, the Baldy Trail is suitable for early- and late-season hiking, when the higher areas of the wilderness are still snowbound.

From the trailhead it is a short distance up the west side of Storm Gulch to where the two trails split; head left here and begin a series of mild switchbacks up a

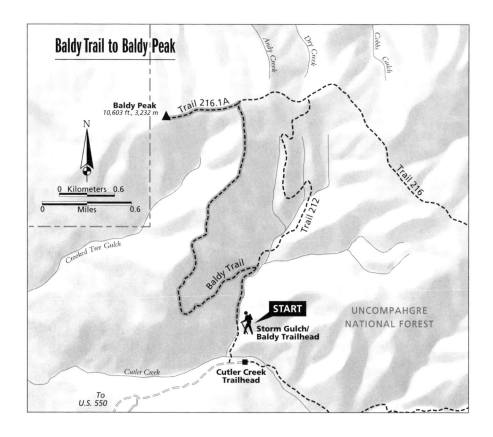

Baldy Trail to Baldy Peak

Baldy Peak
10,603 ft., 3,232 m

Trail 216.1A

Trail 216

Trail 212

Andy Creek

Dry Creek

Cobbs Gulch

Crooked Tree Gulch

Baldy Trail

N

0 Kilometers 0.6
0   Miles   0.6

START
Storm Gulch/
Baldy Trailhead

UNCOMPAHGRE
NATIONAL FOREST

Cutler Creek
Cutler Creek
Trailhead

To
U.S. 550

sunny hillside of oak brush. Traverse to the southwest for approximately a quarter mile to a saddle, then continue west and northwest as the peaks of the Sneffels Range come progressively into view. The trail then begins a more northerly trend and reaches a saddle at approximately 1.8 miles and 9,790 feet of elevation. Fine views make this a good rest spot. Continue up the blunt, gently graded ridgetop to an obvious split in the trail; the right-hand option (Trail 216) follows Baldy Ridge to the south, making connections with the Storm Gulch, Cutler Creek, and Dexter Creek Trails in that order of distance. If you choose one of these connections, keep in mind that there are no water sources along the ridge, and that both the main trail and connecting trails can be quite difficult to find. To complete this day hike, continue west on Trail 216.1A toward the modest summit of Baldy Peak (if the trail is not obvious, just stay near the south edge of the trees). The view from Baldy takes in the West Elk Mountains to the north and La Sal Mountains of Utah to the west, but dominant is the rugged Sneffels Range to the southwest. Retrace your steps to the trailhead to complete the hike.

Scenery from the Baldy Trail.

Options

The ridgetop trail (Trail 216) that connects Baldy and Storm Gulch can be followed southeast for approximately 3 miles to connect with the Cutler Creek Trail (Trail 217.2A or 217, Hike 4), creating a loop hike of approximately 8 miles and ending in Thistle Park. Trail 216 also connects farther to the southeast with the Dexter Creek Trail (loop distance approximately 11 miles; car shuttle required). Considerable route-finding skills may be needed to successfully complete these extended hikes, and there is no water available for a long distance.

7 Stealey Mountain Trail to Stealey Mountain

Forest Service Trail 219

An easy, low-elevation hike mostly outside the wilderness area with impressive views of the west faces of Courthouse Mountain and Chimney Rock, and a high level of solitude.

Type of hike: Day hike.
Distance: 6.5 miles out-and-back (east trailhead).
10.5 miles out-and-back (Vista Point).
Difficulty: Easy.
Trail conditions: Most of this hike takes place on old logging roads, so it tends to be dry and easy to follow. If you continue on the Stealey Mountain Trail beyond the saddle at 2.9 miles, the trail becomes more difficult to find. Water is available only at Owl Creek (0.7 mile from the east trailhead). Informal trailhead camping is permitted at both Vista Point and at the east trailhead, but neither place is equipped with sanitary facilities. Mountain bikes may be encountered, as this hike lies outside the wilderness area.
Maps: USGS Courthouse Mountain 7.5-minute quadrangle.
Management: Ouray Ranger District, Uncompahgre National Forest.

Finding the trailhead: From U.S. Highway 550 find the turnoff to the Owl Creek Pass Road (Ouray County Road 10), located 24.1 miles south of the U.S. Highway 50/U.S. 550 intersection in Montrose and 1.7 miles north of the traffic light in Ridgway. Follow this road toward Owl Creek Pass. Measured from U.S. 550 it is 8.9 miles to the Vista Point Trailhead on the right and 13.2 miles to an unmarked turnoff to the unnamed east trailhead. The east trailhead provides a shorter and much more pleasant approach to this hike, and is strongly recommended over Vista Point. Follow the road from the turnoff for a short distance to a dead end at the trailhead.

Landmarks

Measured from east trailhead:

- **0.0** Stealey Mountain East Trailhead.
- **0.7** Crossing of Owl Creek.
- **2.9** Saddle (fence line and cattleguard).
- **6.5** Stealey Mountain East Trailhead.

The Hike

Although located entirely outside the Uncompahgre Wilderness, this hike is included in this book because it is an easy and pleasant day hike that also provides a possible point of access into the Cow Creek area of the wilderness. Although two different trailheads are described here, the approach via the east trailhead is recommended.

From the east trailhead hike downhill on the roadbed as it bends to the south

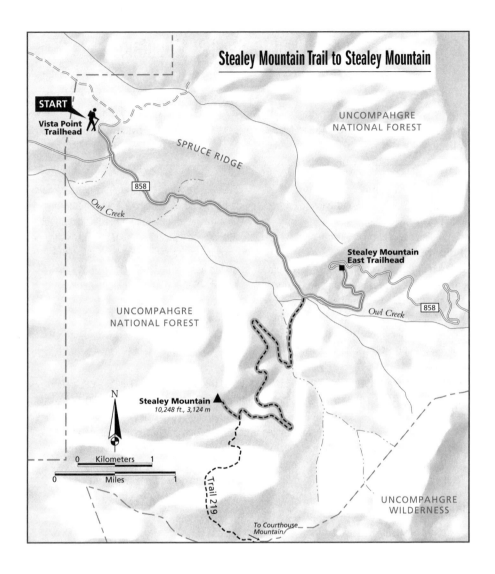

Stealey Mountain Trail to Stealey Mountain

START
Vista Point Trailhead

SPRUCE RIDGE

UNCOMPAHGRE NATIONAL FOREST

858

Owl Creek

Stealey Mountain East Trailhead

Owl Creek

858

UNCOMPAHGRE NATIONAL FOREST

N

Stealey Mountain
10,248 ft., 3,124 m

0   Kilometers   1

0   Miles   1

Trail 219

To Courthouse Mountain

UNCOMPAHGRE WILDERNESS

and southeast. Where the road turns toward the west and approaches Owl Creek, scoot left onto a trail that descends between the road and the creek. Follow this trail down some steep grades, parallel to the creekbed, to an easy stream crossing at 0.7 mile. Pick up a road on the south side of the creek, which soon merges with another roadbed heading south.

To reach the same junction from Vista Point (to repeat—this is not recommended), pick up a trail heading downhill and southeast directly from the turnoff, and improvise through an eroded area. Courthouse Mountain looms above this section, and the Sneffels Range is visible to the southeast. After a quarter mile merge with an old roadbed; follow this left (southeast). At an inside bend, at approximately

1 mile, look sharply for a drop-off to a second, lower roadbed. Lose elevation gradually in the next section, with plenty of shade from aspen groves. The roadbed begins to gain elevation slowly, and the roar of Owl Creek is soon heard. A short section parallel to the creek leads to a crossing, which should not present a problem except perhaps during snowmelt runoff or large thunderstorms. On the south side of the creek, pass a corral-like structure and take a right-hand fork up a roadbed, which soon merges with the trail from the east trailhead.

Note that the USGS Courthouse Mountain quadrangle map is not accurate for the following section of trail. Follow the roadbed generally south until it peters out in a meadow, and head right to an obvious crossing of a small tributary drainage. Rather than becoming a pack trail as shown on the USGS quadrangle map, the roadbed heads up a mild, steady grade to the northwest to a switchback. As the trail turns back to the south, the west faces of Courthouse Mountain and then Chimney Rock come back into view. A few more switchbacks and a steady but mild uphill climb lead to a saddle with an old fence line and cattleguard. The saddle makes a good destination for the day hike, or you can perform a short bushwhack northwest to the unimpressive summit of Stealey Mountain (Green Mountain on the USGS quadrangle map). Although there are nice campsites at the saddle, no water is available for quite a distance.

From the destination simply retrace your steps to the trailhead.

Options

From the destination described here, the Stealey Mountain Trail can be extended into the Cow Creek drainage and the Uncompahgre Wilderness Area via the trail's southern extension or the Courthouse Trail (Trail 218). An extended hike to the east end of the Courthouse Trail, located along the West Fork Road (Cimarron River West Fork), is also possible (this would be the reverse of Hike 8 as described in this book), but the trail is quite obscure and will challenge your route-finding abilities.

8 Courthouse and Stealey Mountain Trails

Forest Service Trails 218 and 219

This is a remote and little-used trail; route-finding and map-reading skills will be required.

Type of hike: Day hike.

Distance: 8 miles point to point.

Difficulty: Moderate.

Trail conditions: Mostly dry. Several sections between the high point on Courthouse Ridge and the saddle near Stealey Mountain are lightly traveled and hard to find. Considerable route-finding ability will be required. If you lose the trail altogether you will need to reverse your course, aiming for a point on the ridgeline located approximately 0.75 mile south of the summit of Courthouse Mountain.

Campsites with water are scarce along the route but are present near both trailheads. The valley of the West Fork of the Cimarron River is a spectacular but heavily used area; please use all available low-impact hiking and camping techniques to protect this area.

Maps: USGS Courthouse Mountain and Dallas 7.5-minute quadrangles; two short sections are located on the north edge of the Wetterhorn Peak quadrangle.

Management: Ouray Ranger District, Uncompahgre National Forest.

Finding the trailhead: There are two approaches to the east trailhead of the Courthouse Trail, located along the West Fork of the Cimarron River. From Montrose and points south to Ouray, approach via U.S. Highway 550. Turn onto the Owl Creek Pass Road (Ouray County Road 10), located 24.1 miles south of the U.S. Highway 50/U.S. 550 intersection in Montrose and 1.7 miles north of the traffic light in Ridgway. Follow this excellent gravel road for approximately 15 miles (see the note below about a shuttle vehicle) over Owl Creek Pass, and turn right at the next intersection.

To reach the same intersection from Montrose and points east, turn south from U.S. 50 toward Silver Jack Reservoir from a point 21.6 miles east of the U.S. 50/U.S. 550 intersection in Montrose and 2.6 miles east of the hamlet of Cimarron. Follow this road 19.5 miles, past the national forest boundary and the Big Cimarron campground, and turn right toward Owl Creek Pass (a left turn heads to the East Fork Trailhead). At another 0.1 mile turn right again (the left road leads to the Middle Fork Trailhead), and at 25.5 miles from U.S. 50 is the above-mentioned intersection. This approach yields commanding views of Chimney Rock, Precipice Peak, Redcliff, and Coxcomb.

From the aforementioned intersection just east of Owl Creek Pass, it is 1.5 miles south to the Courthouse East Trailhead, located by a sign on the west side of the road. Good informal campsites with water (from the West Fork), along with rest rooms, are located in the area near the trailhead.

The north end of the Stealey Mountain Trail is the endpoint of the hike. Leave a shuttle vehicle at an unmarked trailhead (Stealey Mountain East Trailhead) located 13.2 miles from where CR 10 (Owl Creek Pass Road) leaves U.S. 550. Turn right (south) from the Owl Creek Pass Road, follow a gravel road a short distance to a dead end and park.

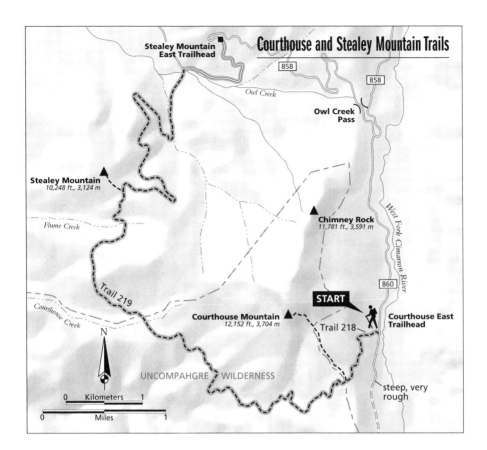

Landmarks

0.0 Courthouse East Trailhead.

0.7 Top of Courthouse Ridge and wilderness boundary.

3.2 Intersect Courthouse Trail (west portion).

5.1 Saddle (fence line and cattleguard).

7.3 Cross Owl Creek.

8.0 Stealey Mountain East Trailhead.

The Hike

The Courthouse Trail, except for the first mile out of the valley of the West Fork of the Cimarron River, is a remote and sparsely traveled route. There is no warm-up on this hike; from the trailhead you begin immediately on a steep and direct climb west toward the ridge that extends south from Courthouse Mountain. This initial portion of the trail is wide and well traveled, and mixes in several stretches that contour south with sections of steeper climbing. After about 650 feet of climbing, the ridgetop and wilderness boundary are reached. The trail heading north along the ridge accesses Courthouse Mountain; however, this hike continues to the west and downhill.

Immediately begin descending steep switchbacks. Pass through several clearings, one of which yields a view of the Sneffels Range, with the trail marked by a post. A larger clearing has the southwest face of Courthouse Mountain looming overhead; the trail briefly disappears here. Do not proceed into the clearing, but rather cut downhill along its south (left, if you are looking downhill) side, where the trail soon reappears and is indicated by several posts (these are not easily visible upon entering the clearing). In case you need to make a return trip to the Courthouse East Trailhead, look for the marker post in the southeastern corner of the clearing marking the trail's point of reentry into the trees.

Continue on a better trail that heads generally west and is marked by old, hard-to-see tree blazes. Hike briefly uphill, turn a corner, and contour into a deep drainage containing surprisingly little water. Climb out of the drainage and contour in a generally southwesterly direction. At a clearing ringed with aspen, the trail again becomes faint, but with care you should be able to follow it through the grass. Pick up the trail heading west from a point near the clearing's lower end. At another clearing, directly below the west face of Courthouse Mountain, the trail disappears yet again. Cross the clearing, staying roughly on contour, and pick up the trail at the clearing's southwest edge. Once again, in case you need to make a return trip to the Courthouse East Trailhead, remember to pick up the trail on the clearing's east side between two low clumps of rock.

A few hundred yards beyond the last clearing described is an inconspicuous, unmarked trail heading south and downhill; this is the southern portion of the Stealey Mountain Trail, which descends south and southwest into the Cow Creek drainage. Do not turn onto this trail, but rather continue straight for a few hundred feet to a flat clearing with a survey marker; the trail cuts sharply to the north here, reentering the trees. The next section of trail is pleasant and shaded as it loops into and out of several small drainages. These are followed by a long, gradual descent to the west; the area had been heavily grazed prior to my visit. Reach a small clearing and a trail junction where the west end of the Courthouse Trail (Trail 218) descends toward Cow Creek.

Take the right-hand trail north, out of the wilderness area, toward Stealey Mountain. A gradual climb to the west-northwest, on an occasionally faint trail, leads to a turn to the north on a better trail. About 1 mile beyond the wilderness boundary and junction with Courthouse Creek, you will turn more to the northeast into the drainage of Flume Creek. A clearing presents a confusing apparent choice of trails, but if you simply follow what appears to be an old roadbed around the Flume Creek drainage, you will reenter the trees on a better trail. Take a turn to the northwest and

The south face of Courthouse Mountain. ▶

Precipice Peak (foreground) viewed from Courthouse Mountain.

crank out a 400-foot climb on a good trail, emerging at a saddle with an old fence line and cattleguard. This is the saddle just southeast of the top of Stealey Mountain.

From the saddle the hike is quite straightforward. Follow an old roadbed as it descends gradually toward Owl Creek. The direction is generally to the north and northeast, albeit with many switchbacks and changes of direction. You will enjoy several fine views of Courthouse Mountain and Chimney Rock as you descend. At an elevation of approximately 9,100 feet, cross a small drainage and enter a meadow that is clearly visible on the USGS Courthouse Mountain quadrangle. Turn north and downhill and pick up the roadbed once again at the north end of the meadow. Follow it downhill and north, taking the right-hand option about 0.4 mile below the meadow. A short distance beyond this, cross to the north side of Owl Creek, then follow a good trail upstream and parallel to the creek. The grade is steep in places, but at 0.3 mile from the creek crossing you will merge with a wide, gently graded roadbed. Follow this for another 0.4 mile to the trailhead and your shuttle vehicle.

$\bigcirc$ Courthouse Mountain
Forest Service Trail 218

An excellent steep hike to an exposed summit with 360-degree views.

Type of hike: Day hike (half day).
Distance: 3 miles out-and-back.
Difficulty: Easy.
Trail conditions: Water and campsites are abundant near the trailhead. The drainage of the West Fork of the Cimarron River is a spectacular but heavily used area; please use all low-impact hiking and camping techniques to protect this area. The trail is well worn and easy to follow.
Maps: USGS Courthouse Mountain 7.5-minute quadrangle.
Management: Ouray Ranger District, Uncompahgre National Forest.

Finding the trailhead: There are two approaches to the east trailhead of the Courthouse Trail, located along the West Fork of the Cimarron River. From Montrose and points south to Ouray, approach via U.S. Highway 550. Turn onto the Owl Creek Pass Road (Ouray County Road 10), located 24.1 miles south of the U.S. Highway 50/U.S. 550 intersection (Main Street and Townsend Avenue) in Montrose and 1.7 miles north of the traffic light in Ridgway. Follow this excellent gravel road for approximately 15 miles over Owl Creek Pass, and turn right at the next intersection.

To reach the same intersection from Montrose and points east, turn south from U.S. 50 toward Silver Jack Reservoir from a point 21.6 miles east of the U.S. 50/U.S. 550 intersection in Montrose and 2.6 miles east of the hamlet of Cimarron. Follow this road 19.5 miles, past the national forest boundary and the Big Cimarron campground, and turn right toward Owl Creek Pass (a left turn heads to the East Fork Trailhead). At another 0.1 mile turn right again (the left road leads to the Middle Fork Trailhead), and at 25.5 miles from U.S. 50 is the above-mentioned intersection. This approach yields commanding views of Chimney Rock, Precipice Peak, Redcliff, and Coxcomb.

From the aforementioned intersection it is 1.5 miles south to the Courthouse East Trailhead, located by a sign on the west side of the road. Good informal campsites with water (from the West Fork), along with rest rooms, are located in the area near the trailhead.

Landmarks

0.0 Courthouse East Trailhead.
0.7 Top of Courthouse Ridge and wilderness boundary.
1.2 Saddle at top of tree-lined corridor.
1.5 Courthouse Mountain.
3.0 Courthouse East Trailhead.

The Hike

Courthouse Mountain is really more than an easy hike because of its considerable steepness and exposure, but its short length makes it accessible to most hikers. A

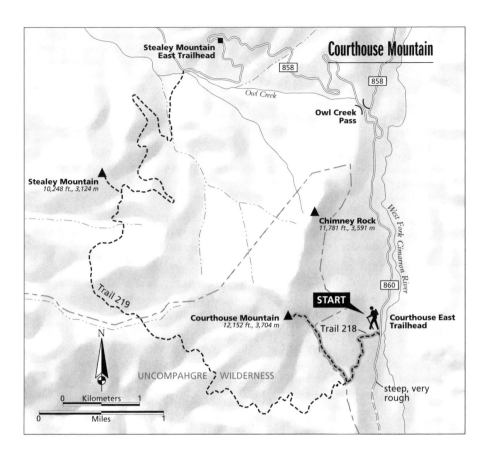

speedy hiker can complete the round trip in about two hours. Not a subtle trail, it climbs steeply nearly from start to finish and yields fine views of the volcanic terrain around the West Fork Valley. This is a popular hike, so be prepared for some company on a fine summer day.

From the Courthouse East Trailhead along the West Fork Road, begin a steep and direct climb toward the ridge south of Courthouse Mountain. The steep climb is broken by a couple of stretches that contour to the south before shooting uphill once again. After about 0.7 mile and 650 feet of climbing, the ridgetop and wilderness boundary are reached. An obvious trail heads north (right) along the ridge, gaining elevation gradually as it winds just east of and below the ridgetop. The trail has become braided along the ridge, so try your best to take the most-traveled line. Occasional views open up of the peaks to the south and of the 800-foot south face of Courthouse Mountain. The grade soon steepens as you enter a tree-lined corridor at about 11,400 feet. The trail up the corridor is steep and dusty, and some sure-footedness will help in places. A saddle at the top of the corridor features a stunning view of Chimney Rock and the ridge of the Cimarron Needles (Turret Ridge) to the north; save some film for this vantage point.

Head left (west) and uphill from the saddle, along a narrow ridgetop. This section is also steep and dusty. Go right, around a 40-foot-high rock band and straight up a gully, then clamber up over ledges of volcanic conglomerate. A short grassy section leads to talus blocks; angle right around some large blocks, following cairns if they are present. File this sequence of features away for use during the return trip. Step up through a short notch, and the summit is just above.

The summit of Courthouse Mountain presents a 360-degree view of the following peaks, starting at the east and working clockwise: Sheep Mountain, Dunsinane Mountain, Precipice Peak, Uncompahgre Peak, Point 13,241, Redcliff, Coxcomb, Point 13,874, Wildhorse Peak, the Sneffels Range, the Uncompahgre Plateau to the west (with Ridgway Reservoir in front), Grand Mesa (in the distance to the north), the West Elk Mountains, and the Turret Ridge. The trail is easy to follow on the return trip.

Chimney Rock from high on Courthouse Mountain.

10 Point 13,241

Forest Service Trail 226

A relatively easy but spectacular peak hike.

Type of hike: Day hike.
Distance: 6.4 miles out-and-back.
Difficulty: Moderate.
Trail conditions: Most of this hike is off-trail but not terribly difficult. Some mountain route-finding skills are useful; remember your land-marks for the return trip to the trailhead.

Maps: USGS Courthouse Mountain and Wetterhorn Peak 7.5-minute quadrangles.
Management: Ouray Ranger District, Uncompahgre National Forest.

Finding the trailhead: There are two approaches to the trailhead, located along the West Fork of the Cimarron River. From Montrose and points south to Ouray, approach via U.S. Highway 550. Turn onto the Owl Creek Pass Road (Ouray County Road 10), located 24.1 miles south of the U.S. Highway 50/U.S. 550 intersection in Montrose and 1.7 miles north of the traffic light in Ridgway. Follow this excellent gravel road for 15 miles over Owl Creek Pass, and turn right at the next intersection.

To reach the same intersection from Montrose and points east, turn south from U.S. 50 toward Silver Jack Reservoir from a point 21.6 miles east of the U.S. 50/U.S. 550 intersection in Montrose and 2.6 miles east of Cimarron. Follow this road 19.5 miles, past the national forest boundary and Big Cimarron campground, and turn right toward Owl Creek Pass (a left turn heads to the East Fork Trailhead). At another 0.1 mile turn right again, and at 25.5 miles is the above-mentioned intersection. This approach yields commanding views of Chimney Rock, Precipice Peak, Redcliff, and Coxcomb.

Another 2.4 miles on the West Fork Road leads to a sign saying NARROW VERY ROUGH ROAD. Passenger cars will want to park here, though high-clearance four-wheel-drive vehicles can continue past a crossing of the West Fork for another mile to the designated trailhead.

Landmarks

0.0 NARROW VERY ROUGH ROAD sign.
0.3 Crossing of West Fork.
1.0 Signed West Fork Trailhead.
1.6 Wilderness boundary.
2.1 Leave the Wetterhorn Basin Trail.
3.0 Saddle on ridge.
3.2 Point 13,241.
6.4 NARROW VERY ROUGH ROAD sign.

The Hike

Point 13,241 is not at all a nameless summit sitting among superior peaks, but rather

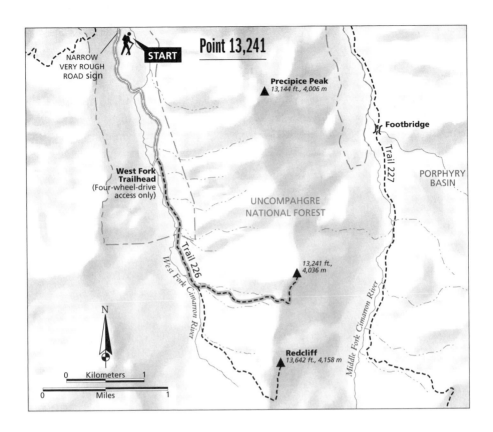

a major high point on the towering ridge that extends north from Coxcomb, between the West Fork and Middle Fork of the Cimarron River. It is a very accessible and beautiful peak climb on which you are sure to find solitude only a short distance from the crowded West Fork Trailhead. Note that the route described is only one of several possible variations to the summit.

From the NARROW VERY ROUGH ROAD sign, drive or hike up the West Fork Road to the crossing of the West Fork. The crossing should not be difficult, either on foot or in a competent vehicle, except during high-water conditions. After the crossing follow the roadbed mostly through a scenic open meadow to the trailhead. The wilderness boundary is soon passed, and the trail begins to climb more steadily in the trees below the northwest flank of Point 13,241. Below timberline you will pass over several usually dry drainages that obviously carry tremendous amounts of sediment during periods of high runoff. If the trail is obscured by recent mudflow, just continue on a bearing slightly to the east of south and pick up the trail once again in the trees.

Continue to a clearing on the trail, located almost below the low point of the saddle between Point 13,241 and Redcliff, and locate the two largest drainages that descend from below the saddle. Hike into the area between the drainages, and ascend into the area where the trees climb highest on the mountainside. At timberline you should be more or less below the low point of the saddle. Above timberline try to note landmarks from above in order to easily retrace your route down from the summit. Head up a grassy slope, bear right below a low cliff band, and work your way up talus and scree between several towers of rock. Above the towers angle left on a vegetated slope to the saddle, which opens up a dramatic view down into the valley of the Middle Fork. From the saddle steep hiking and some scrambling gains the summit. From the top of Point 13,241, retrace your route back to your vehicle.

10 Redcliff
Forest Service Trail 226

A relatively accessible peak hike with commanding views of the high peaks of the Uncompahgre.

Type of hike: Day hike.
Distance: 8.4 miles out-and-back.
Difficulty: Difficult.
Trail conditions: Redcliff involves strenuous off-trail hiking, but route finding is not difficult.

Maps: USGS Courthouse Mountain and Wetterhorn Peak 7.5-minute quadrangles.
Management: Ouray Ranger District, Uncompahgre National Forest.

Finding the trailhead: There are two approaches to the trailhead, located along the West Fork of the Cimarron River. From Montrose and points south to Ouray, approach via U.S. Highway 550. Turn onto the Owl Creek Pass Road (Ouray County Road 10), located 24.1 miles south of the U.S. Highway 50/U.S. 550 intersection in Montrose and 1.7 miles north of the traffic light in Ridgway. Follow this excellent gravel road for 15 miles over Owl Creek Pass and turn right at the next intersection.

To reach the same intersection from Montrose and points east, turn south from U.S. 50 toward Silver Jack Reservoir from a point 21.6 miles east of the U.S. 50/U.S. 550 intersection in Montrose and 2.6 miles east of Cimarron. Follow this road 19.5 miles, past the national forest boundary and Big Cimarron campground, and turn right toward Owl Creek Pass (a left turn heads to the East Fork Trailhead). At another 0.1 mile turn right again, and at 25.5 miles is the above-mentioned intersection. This approach yields commanding views of Chimney Rock, Precipice Peak, Redcliff, and Coxcomb.

Another 2.4 miles on the West Fork Road leads to a sign saying NARROW VERY ROUGH ROAD. Passenger cars will want to park here, though high-clearance four-wheel-drive vehicles can continue past a crossing of the West Fork for another mile to the designated trailhead.

Landmarks

0.0 NARROW VERY ROUGH ROAD sign.

0.3 Crossing of West Fork.

1.0 Signed West Fork Trailhead.

1.6 Wilderness boundary.

2.5 Leave the Wetterhorn Basin Trail.

3.7 Saddle on ridge.

4.2 Redcliff.

8.4 NARROW VERY ROUGH ROAD sign.

The Hike

Redcliff is one of the highest peaks in the Uncompahgre Wilderness, and as such its

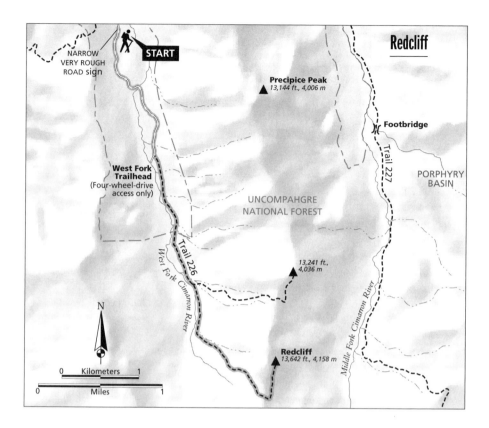

Within the map:

NARROW VERY ROUGH ROAD sign

START

Precipice Peak
13,144 ft., 4,006 m

Footbridge

West Fork Trailhead
(Four-wheel-drive access only)

Trail 227

PORPHYRY BASIN

UNCOMPAHGRE NATIONAL FOREST

Trail 226

West Fork Cimarron River

13,241 ft., 4,036 m

N

Middle Fork Cimarron River

Redcliff
13,642 ft., 4,158 m

0   Kilometers   1

0   Miles   1

summit gives commanding views in all directions. This hike involves a relatively simple but strenuous variation on the Wetterhorn Basin Trail. The route described is only one of several that are possible; by leaving the Wetterhorn Basin Trail at a higher point, you can reduce the steepness of the hike while adding somewhat to its distance.

From the NARROW VERY ROUGH ROAD sign, drive or hike up the West Fork Road to the crossing of the West Fork. The crossing should not be difficult except during high-water conditions. After the crossing follow the roadbed mostly through a scenic open meadow to the designated trailhead. Beyond the trailhead the wilderness boundary is soon passed, and the trail begins to climb more steadily in the trees below the northwest flank of Point 13,241. Below timberline you will pass over several usually dry drainages that obviously carry tremendous amounts of sediment during periods of high runoff. If the trail is obscured by recent mudflow, just continue on a bearing slightly to the east of south and pick up the trail once again in the trees.

Continue on the Wetterhorn Basin Trail past a section that closely follows the bank of the West Fork. Leave the trail at a clearing (at just under 11,400 feet) just below timberline and just upstream from the drainage that descends the west face of Redcliff. Cruise up mostly grassy slopes to a flatter area at approximately 12,100 feet. Note the 150-foot cliff located down and right of the much higher cliffs making up the upper west face of Redcliff. Angle up and right (roughly south-southeast) around the 150-foot cliff, then angle left above its right side, going left of the cliff-band (which is lengthier but not as tall) that extends under the north face of Cox-comb. Arrive at the Coxcomb-Redcliff saddle just above, and there are no obstacles from the saddle to Redcliff's summit. The view in all directions is spectacular, taking in all of the major peaks of the Uncompahgre and beyond. Return to your vehicle on West Fork by retracing your route.

12 Wetterhorn Basin Trail

Forest Service Trail 226

Mostly above timberline, this hike offers spectacular views of Dunsinane Mountain, Precipice Peak, Redcliff, Coxcomb, and Wetterhorn Peak, along with superb wildflowers in season.

Type of hike: Day hike or two-day backpack.
Distance: 7.6 miles out-and-back (Wetterhorn Pass).
10.6 miles out-and-back (Wetterhorn Basin).
Difficulty: Moderate (Wetterhorn Pass). Difficult (Wetterhorn Basin).
Trail conditions: Water and campsites are abundant near the trailhead, north of Wetterhorn Pass, and near Wetterhorn Creek. The drainage of the West Fork of the Cimarron River is a spectacular but heavily used area; please use all available low-impact hiking and camping techniques to protect this area.
Maps: USGS Courthouse Mountain and Wetterhorn Peak 7.5-minute quadrangles.
Management: Ouray Ranger District, Uncompahgre National Forest.

Finding the trailhead: There are two approaches to the trailhead, located along the West Fork of the Cimarron River. From Montrose and points south to Ouray, approach via U.S. Highway 550. Turn onto the Owl Creek Pass Road (Ouray County Road 10), located 24.1 miles south of the U.S. 50/U.S. 550 intersection (Main Street and Townsend Avenue) in Montrose and 1.7 miles north of the traffic light in Ridgway. Follow this excellent gravel road for 15 miles over Owl Creek Pass and turn right at the next intersection.

To reach the same intersection from Montrose and points east, turn south from U.S. 50 toward Silver Jack Reservoir from a point 21.6 miles east of the U.S. 50/U.S. 550 intersection in Montrose and 2.6 miles east of Cimarron. Follow this road 19.5 miles, past the national forest boundary and Big Cimarron campground, and turn right toward Owl Creek Pass (a left turn heads to the East Fork Trailhead). At another 0.1 mile turn right again (the left road leads to the Middle Fork Trailhead), and at 25.5 miles is the above-mentioned intersection. This approach yields commanding views of Chimney Rock, Precipice Peak, Redcliff, and Coxcomb.

Another 2.4 miles on the West Fork Road leads to a sign saying NARROW VERY ROUGH ROAD. Passenger cars will want to park here, though high-clearance four-wheel-drive vehicles can continue past a crossing of the West Fork for another mile to the designated trailhead.

Landmarks

- **0.0** NARROW VERY ROUGH ROAD sign.
- **0.3** Crossing of West Fork.
- **1.0** Signed West Fork Trailhead.
- **1.6** Wilderness boundary.
- **3.8** Wetterhorn Pass.

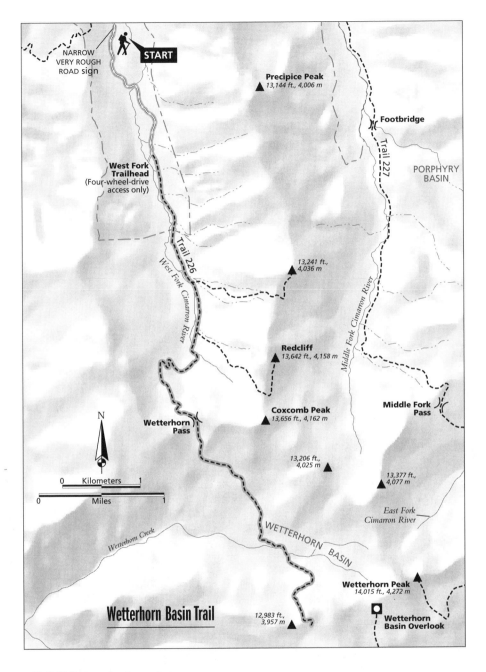

(5.1) Wetterhorn Creek crossing.

(5.3) Second pass above Wetterhorn Basin.

7.6 (10.6) NARROW VERY ROUGH ROAD sign.

The Hike

Wetterhorn Pass is an informal name used in this book to refer to the prominent saddle that sits at the upper (south) end of the drainage of the West Fork of the Cimarron River. On a half-day hike to the pass, you will see fantastic wildflower meadows and some of the most rugged alpine terrain in the Uncompahgre. The picturesque Wetterhorn Basin sits high on the west flank of Wetterhorn Peak, south of Wetterhorn Pass, and provides a rigorous day hike or a relatively easy-to-reach destination for an overnight trip. Whether followed all the way into Wetterhorn Basin or just to the pass, this trail is my own favorite day hike in the Uncompahgre Wilderness.

The view north from Wetterhorn Pass. Courthouse Mountain in the distance.

Precipice Peak from the Wetterhorn Basin Trail.

From the NARROW VERY ROUGH ROAD sign, hike or continue to drive up the rough West Fork Road. Bear left at 0.2 mile and cross the creek very soon after. The crossing should be no problem on foot or in a competent four-wheel-drive vehicle except during very high-water periods. Beyond the crossing the route is obvious and easy to follow on a roadbed through a large meadow. The designated trailhead and wilderness boundary are soon passed, and the trail begins to climb more steadily in the trees below the northwest flank of Point 13,241. Below timberline you will pass over several usually dry drainages that obviously carry tremendous amounts of sediment during periods of high runoff. If the trail is obscured by recent mudflow, just continue on a bearing slightly to the east of south and pick up the trail once again in the trees. As you proceed to near timberline, the wildflowers along the creekbed combine with the rugged peaks above to produce visual overload.

Above timberline the trail wanders considerably more than is shown on the USGS Wetterhorn Peak topographic map, meandering far into the west side of the valley. This area is dense with wildflowers and large boulders that have been shed from the mountain walls above, and the trail climbs steadily through this section. The last steep stretch below Wetterhorn Pass has at least one section that is steep and crumbly; use care here, especially if wearing a heavy pack.

The pass makes a fine destination for a moderate day hike. To fully enjoy the view, however, you should climb for a few minutes up the mountainside to the west-southwest for a stunning view of Wetterhorn Peak. If you are continuing into Wetterhorn Basin, begin dropping downhill to the south on a good trail, meeting up before long with a streambed. Approximately a quarter mile below the pass, the trail levels out and bends more to the southeast as the imposing west face of Wetterhorn Peak increasingly dominates the view. The trail continues, indistinctly in places, downhill and to the southeast as it approaches Wetterhorn Creek. As you near the creek, there is some flat ground on which to pitch a tent, but if you desire some tree cover you will have to follow the creek west and downstream for approximately a quarter mile.

Options

From Wetterhorn Basin it is possible but rather difficult to hike out to the south side of the Uncompahgre Wilderness, toward Mary Alice Creek, via a route shown on the Trails Illustrated map. This is not recommended, however, due to difficult terrain and the lack of an established trail.

13 Middle Fork Trail to Middle Fork Pass

Forest Service Trail 227

Wildflowers; views of Coxcomb, Redcliff, Uncompahgre Peak, Wetterhorn Peak, and others.

Type of hike: Day hike.
Distance: 11.2 miles out-and-back.
Difficulty: Difficult.
Trail conditions: The Middle Fork Trail is extremely well maintained, and in normal conditions will be dry and easy to follow. The trail appears to receive relatively heavy use but is still far from crowded. Approximately 2 miles of the trail lies above timberline and is therefore subject to the typical associated weather dangers—especially high wind and lightning.
Maps: USGS Courthouse Mountain and Wetterhorn Peak 7.5-minute quadrangles.
Management: Ouray Ranger District, Uncompahgre National Forest.

Finding the trailhead: The Middle Fork Trailhead is located up a bumpy road from its intersection with the West Fork and East Fork Roads, about 2 miles above Silver Jack Reservoir. To reach this point from Montrose and points east, turn south from U.S. Highway 50 toward Silver Jack Reservoir from a point 21.6 miles east of the U.S. 50/U.S. 550 intersection in Montrose and 2.6 miles east of Cimarron. Follow this road 19.5 miles, past the national forest boundary and Big Cimarron campground, and turn right toward Owl Creek Pass (a left turn heads to the East Fork Trailhead). At another 0.1 mile turn left onto the Middle Fork Road. From this last turn it is 4.7 bumpy miles to the trailhead. The same point can be reached from near Ridgway by taking the Owl Creek Pass Road (Ouray County Road 10), located 24.1 miles south of the U.S. 50/U.S. 550 intersection (Main Street and Townsend Avenue) in Montrose and 1.7 miles north of the traffic light in Ridgway. Follow this excellent gravel road for 15 miles over Owl Creek Pass, and turn left at the next intersection. The Middle Fork Road is well marked as it departs to the right approximately 6 miles later.

Most passenger cars should be able to negotiate the Middle Fork Road. The road is quite rocky, however, and during wet weather it is not uncommon for small mudslides and debris flows to block the road in several places; having a high-clearance four-wheel-drive vehicle along will provide some insurance against being stuck until the road is cleared. The trailhead area has plenty of room for dispersed camping, but has no sanitary facilities. The area receives fairly heavy use, so please try to minimize your impact if camping here.

Landmarks

0.0 Middle Fork Trailhead.
0.25 Wilderness boundary.
2.2 Footbridge over Porphyry Creek.
4.1 Sharp turn to southeast.
5.6 Middle Fork Pass.
11.2 Middle Fork Trailhead.

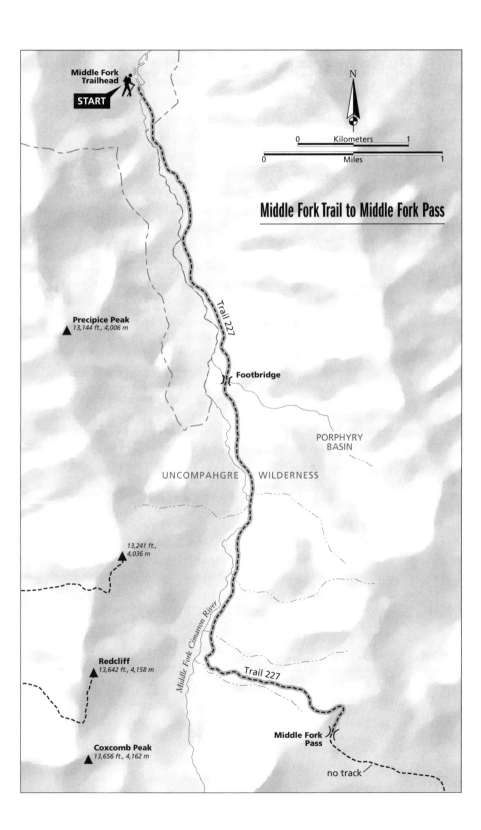

Middle Fork
Trailhead
START

N

0 Kilometers 1
0 Miles 1

Middle Fork Trail to Middle Fork Pass

Trail 227

Footbridge

PORPHYRY
BASIN

▲ Precipice Peak
13,144 ft., 4,006 m

UNCOMPAHGRE WILDERNESS

13,241 ft.,
4,036 m

Middle Fork Cimarron River

Redcliff
▲ 13,642 ft., 4,158 m

Trail 227

Middle Fork
Pass

Coxcomb Peak
▲ 13,656 ft., 4,162 m

no track

The Hike

Along with its neighbor the Wetterhorn Basin Trail (in the West Fork of the Cimarron River), the Middle Fork of the Cimarron is one of my favorite day hikes in the Uncompahgre Wilderness. A well-maintained and relatively easy trail leads up the east side of the Middle Fork of the Cimarron River into a meadow near timberline that is characterized by dramatic mountain views and a wonderful variety of wildflowers. The more ambitious hiker will want to continue up the final 1,200-foot climb to Middle Fork Pass, from which views of many of the Uncompahgre's high peaks reward the hard work.

The first 1.5 miles or so is a veritable "freeway" of a trail, with few loose or muddy sections to slow you down. Near the 2-mile mark, the trail steepens and climbs to a point well above the creek. At just over 2 miles, a good-sized tributary creek descends from Porphyry Basin to the east; a rough trail departs here for the basin. Cross the tributary and climb rather steeply out its south side, through switch-

Coxcomb Peak above the Middle Fork Trail.

backs, to where it levels out once again. Pass through a couple of areas of heavy timber fall and a very nice, cruisy, 0.8-mile section of trail.

At about 3.5 miles from the trailhead, you enter the meadow that makes up the upper part of the Middle Fork drainage and is the visual highlight of the hike. Wonderful views of Coxcomb, Redcliff, and various unnamed peaks compete with a stunning variety of wildflowers for your attention. Many hikers turn around here, but the best is yet to come. After a narrow stretch of trail just above the river is an apparent split in the track; the slightly higher course presents a more obvious trail, but the two come back together in a few hundred yards in either case. In the upper part of the meadow, the trail remains well above (east of) the creek. Pass through some pockets of tree cover (good campsites for those continuing into the East Fork) and begin climbing more steeply just before the eastward turn that characterizes the upper part of this hike.

After turning to the east and uphill, an excellent trail leads into the flower-filled upper basin. The trail fades out near the 12,000-foot contour, but marker posts lead the way (in foggy weather these may be difficult to find). The final climb of 300 feet is negotiated by way of a long switchback. From Middle Fork Pass the view takes in (from east-southeast through the south and west) Uncompahgre Peak, the saddle where the East Fork and El Paso Creek Trails join, Matterhorn Peak (connected to Wetterhorn via a jagged ridge), Wetterhorn Peak, Point 13,411 just above the pass, Coxcomb, Redcliff, Point 13,241, Precipice Peak, and Dunsinane Mountain. To return to the trailhead, head back down through the basin and along the east side of the Middle Fork of the Cimarron.

Options

This hike is commonly extended into the East Fork drainage to the East Fork Trailhead, described as Hike 28 in this book.

Flowers and waterfall along the Middle Fork Trail.

14 Little Cimarron Trail to Sheep Mountain

Forest Service Trail 229

A remote and visually prominent thirteener with a high level of solitude.

Type of hike: Long day hike or overnight backpack.

Distance: 11.2 miles out-and-back.

Difficulty: Difficult.

Trail conditions: Some fallen timber can be expected. Once you leave the main Little Cimarron Trail, there is only occasionally a good track to follow.

Maps: USGS Sheep Mountain 7.5-minute quadrangle.

Management: Ouray Ranger District, Uncompahgre National Forest.

Finding the trailhead: From U.S. Highway 50, turn south onto a dirt road signed LITTLE CIMARRON ROAD. The turnoff is located 41.1 miles west of the intersection of U.S. 50 and Colorado Highway 135 in Gunnison and 22.9 miles east of the intersection of U.S. 50 and U.S. 550 (the corner of Main and Townsend) in Montrose. Follow the Little Cimarron Road (a little rough in places but easily passable by passenger cars) for 15.6 miles to a small road that cuts down and right. This is the Little Cimarron Trailhead, which presents the best trailhead camping in the area and is one of two possible starting points for the hike. It is suggested instead (whether camping at Little Cimarron or not) that you start the hike 0.4 mile farther up the Little Cimarron Road at the hairpin turn that constitutes the Little Cimarron East Trailhead. This trailhead makes the hike a bit shorter and much easier despite adding a river crossing; the hike will be described from the east trailhead.

If you wish to spread this trip over more than one day, campsites with reliable water supplies are not difficult to find throughout the first 4 miles of the hike.

Landmarks

0.0 Little Cimarron East Trailhead.

1.4 Cross Little Cimarron River.

2.7 Wilderness boundary.

4.2 Begin steep uphill climb.

5.6 Sheep Mountain.

11.2 Little Cimarron East Trailhead.

The Hike

The summit of Sheep Mountain is highly sought after by Colorado peak baggers, as it is a prominent mountain when viewed from any direction. Beginning from the more easterly of the Little Cimarron Trailheads will cut the distance and difficulty of this hike down to size—though it still involves 3,700 feet of elevation gain. Begin hiking on an old roadbed at an almost imperceptible grade. The first 1.4 miles of trail,

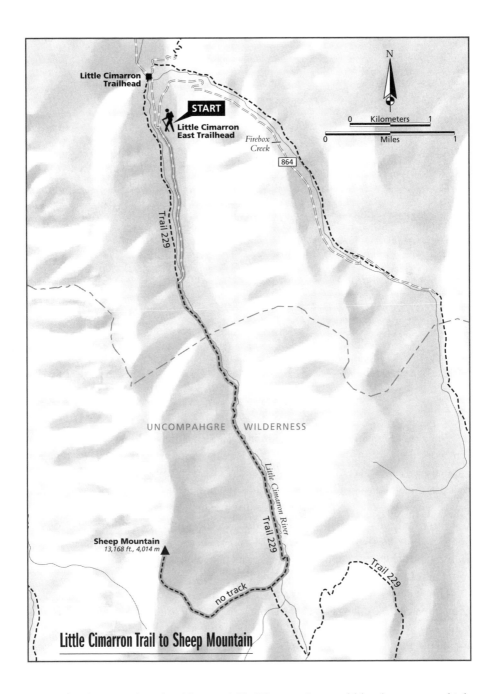

Little Cimarron Trail to Sheep Mountain

up to the river crossing, should go quickly. The crossing could be dangerous at high water; under these conditions you may have to retreat and start from the main Little Cimarron Trailhead. From the crossing it is only a few minutes to where you will merge with the main trail.

Bill Crick in a meadow along the Little Cimarron Trail. Photo: Cathy Crick

Once on the main trail, it is only about 0.3 mile to the wilderness boundary. The trail continues south, parallel to the Little Cimarron, at one point climbing to approximately 150 feet above the river. You will pass through at least five clearings that descend from the east face of Sheep Mountain; these are enormous chutes that have been carved out by frequent wintertime avalanches. At a point just over 4 miles from the trailhead, the trail will bend more to the southwest into the base of yet another chute descending from Sheep Mountain. If you look carefully, portions of a faint trail may be visible above you; this is the chute you will climb to reach the summit. The easiest line probably lies on the left (south) side of the clearing.

This is a very steep climb, as you will gain more than 2,000 feet of elevation in approximately 1.2 miles. The route is obvious enough: Above the point where the chute reaches timberline, you will take the easiest path up the southeast flank of the mountain. The 13,168-foot summit is reached abruptly, and is really the south end of a tilted plateau that drops off to the north. Enjoy wonderful views of Silver Mountain to the south and Precipice Peak, Redcliff, Coxcomb, Wetterhorn, and Uncompahgre Peaks to the west, southwest, and south. Because much of the summit plateau is bounded by steep, unstable ground, resist the urge to find a shorter route back to the trailhead. Retrace your steps down the southeast side of the mountain and down the Little Cimarron Trail.

15 Fall Creek Trail

Forest Service Trail 231

A long hike with plenty of gentle high–alpine scenery.

Type of hike: Day hike, although it can be combined with other trails for a fine two- to three-day backpacking outing.

Distance: 12 miles out-and-back (to junction with Little Cimarron Trail).

13.4 miles out-and-back (to saddle east of Silver Mountain).

Difficulty: Moderate.

Trail conditions: Several sections of the trail tend to be wet and boggy. There are two stream crossings; plan on wet feet at the first except during low-water conditions. The trail appears to receive moderate to heavy horse traffic. The upper basin may be grazed by sheep during midsummer. Campsites with available water are abundant.

Maps: USGS Sheep Mountain and Uncompahgre Peak 7.5-minute quadrangles.

Management: Ouray and Gunnison Ranger Districts, Uncompahgre National Forest.

Finding the trailhead: From U.S. Highway 50, turn south onto a dirt road signed LITTLE CIMAR-RON ROAD. The turnoff is located 41.1 miles west of the intersection of U.S. 50 and Colorado Highway 135 in Gunnison and 22.9 miles east of the intersection of U.S. 50 and U.S. 550 in Montrose. Follow the Little Cimarron Road (a little rough in places but easily passable by passenger cars) for 20.1 miles, past the Little Cimarron (recommended for camping) and Little Cimarron East Trailheads, to the Fall Creek Trailhead on the right. Trailhead camping is possible at Fall Creek, but the Little Cimarron Trailhead (5 miles back down the road) is much roomier and is highly recommended.

Landmarks

0.0 Fall Creek Trailhead.

1.8 Firebox Creek/Fall Creek divide.

2.1 First stream crossing.

3.9 Second stream crossing.

6.0 Junction with Little Cimarron Trail; turn left (south).

6.7 Saddle above Fall Creek between Point 13,051 and Silver Mountain.

12.0 (13.4) Fall Creek Trailhead.

The Hike

The Fall Creek Trail starts at a high elevation of approximately 11,000 feet, thereby giving relatively easy access to the high country in the heart of the Uncompahgre Wilderness. The hiking is enjoyable, with no big climbs, for about the first 5.5 miles. Begin by hiking briefly downhill from the southwest side of the trailhead parking area. The wilderness boundary is reached almost immediately as the trail enters a

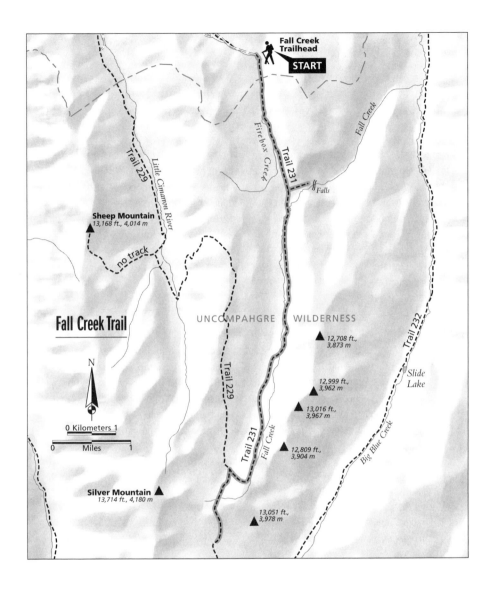

Fall Creek Trailhead
START

Fall Creek

Firebox Creek

Trail 231

Falls

Trail 229

Little Cinnamon River

Sheep Mountain
13,168 ft., 4,014 m

no track

Fall Creek Trail

UNCOMPAHGRE WILDERNESS

N

0 Kilometers 1
0 Miles 1

Trail 229

Trail 231

Fall Creek

Silver Mountain ▲
13,714 ft., 4,180 m

13,051 ft.,
3,978 m

12,809 ft.,
3,904 m

13,016 ft.,
3,967 m

12,999 ft.,
3,962 m

12,708 ft.,
3,873 m

Trail 232

Slide
Lake

Big Blue Creek

wide meadow along Firebox Creek. Climb briefly up a low hill, with an even more brief downhill stretch behind it, and enter a beautiful, wide meadow. The flat and easy trail continues up the east side of the meadow to another brief climb and a short, moderate descent. It is on this second descent that you will pass into the drainage of Fall Creek, which bends to the east near this point, passes over a waterfall, and descends northeast into Big Blue Creek. From the base of the short downhill section of trail, a 0.2-mile side trip to the east makes a popular day-hike destination (approximately 2 miles one-way). From the waterfall is a fine view into Big Blue Creek and the high ridge beyond. To continue up Fall Creek, take the trail to the south to the first stream crossing at 2.1 miles. The crossing will present no particular difficulty except during periods of very high runoff.

For the next 1.5 miles, the trail simply follows the east side of a huge, beautiful meadow. It may become boggy and difficult to follow in a few spots, but stay on a heading almost directly south, and stay east of the creek. During this stretch the Fall Creek–Big Blue saddle (the uppermost portions of the trail continue over this into the drainage of Big Blue Creek) comes progressively into view to the south. Note that, although well below tree line, this meadow is exposed and should be avoided if possible during thunderstorms. For those planning a loop hike via the Little Cimarron Trail as described in Hike 29, the upper part of the Little Cimarron is located on top of the ridge that lies directly to the west.

The meadow gradually narrows, and you reach the second creek crossing at 3.9 miles; those looking for an easy day hike might consider turning around here. On the west side of the crossing, the trail begins to climb steadily but not steeply. The

Near timberline on the Fall Creek Trail.

track becomes faint in one grassy section, but it is obvious where it reenters the trees. The next section of trail, near the south border of the USGS Sheep Mountain quadrangle, climbs steadily under tree cover and is likely to be muddy in several places. This section also passes through several avalanche runout zones, which could make for difficult or even dangerous hiking conditions during the early season.

The last major stand of trees has some small but well-sheltered possible campsites. Above tree line, in an open flowered meadow, the trail actually loses about 150 feet of elevation, but it soon regains its steady uphill course. Several small tributary drainages provide water here if needed. Above is a flat spot with the remains of a small wooden structure. At times during the summer, this area serves as a high camp for sheepherders; be prepared to encounter sheep and/or people in the area. This is another good spot to turn around if you have had enough for the day.

From the flat spot the trail becomes indistinct; head to the south-southwest for a few hundred feet to once again pick up the trail, which soon angles back uphill to the northwest. The trail junction with the Little Cimarron is approximately at the toe (lowest point) of the large scree field at the base of the craggy peak to the west. From the trail junction you can angle steeply uphill to the northwest on the Little Cimarron Trail to the ridgetop, or you can head south toward the saddle leading into Big Blue Creek (the high point of the Fall Creek Trail). From the three-way trail junction, head south for about 0.8 mile, aiming for a high saddle between Point 13,051 to the east and Silver Mountain to the west. During the early and middle summer, there may be snowbanks to contend with, but these pose no particular difficulty. If you are hiking only for the day, you will almost surely wish to turn around here, 6.7 miles and 2,600 vertical feet from the trailhead.

Options

The Fall Creek Trail can be combined with any of several other trails to create two- to three-day backpacking outings ending at another trailhead. The Fall Creek/Little Cimarron combination is most compelling, and is described in this book (Hike 29). From Fall Creek the south end of the Big Blue Trail (Trail 232) can also be used to access trailheads in the southern part of the Uncompahgre, near Uncompahgre Peak.

16 Big Blue Trail to Slide Lake and Beyond
Forest Service Trail 232

Fine fishing and a relatively easy trail.

Type of hike: Day hike.
Distance: 10.4 miles out-and-back.
Difficulty: Moderate.
Trail conditions: The trail is mostly wide, dry, and easy to follow, with relatively few obstacles such as downed timber. Water is readily available throughout its length. Slide Lake at 5 miles is a justifiably popular area to fish and camp, but it is recommended that you camp well away from the lake—this is a heavily used area. If you do camp at Slide Lake, please tread lightly.
Maps: USGS Sheep Mountain and Uncompahgre Peak 7.5-minute quadrangles.
Management: Gunnison Ranger District, Uncompahgre National Forest.

Finding the trailhead: The Big Blue Trailhead is located just outside the wilderness boundary in the northeastern part of the area, and there are two vehicle approaches. The first approach is best if you are starting your trip from Gunnison or the eastern side of the Uncompahgre. From Colorado Highway 149, 11 miles north of Lake City or 33.6 miles south of the U.S. Highway 50/CO 149 intersection west of Gunnison, turn west onto the Alpine Road. The first 5 miles is quite narrow and rough but passable in most passenger cars, and leads to an intersection with the Alpine Plateau Road.

From Montrose and the western side of the Uncompahgre, use either the approach above or the Alpine Plateau Road approach. Turn south from U.S. 50 onto the well-marked Alpine Plateau Road, 33.9 miles west of Gunnison and 30.6 miles east of Montrose. The road is long and rough but passable in most passenger cars. It forks several times, but signs to Big Blue Campground should help keep you on track. From U.S. 50 it is a slow 21.1 miles to the intersection with the Alpine Road.

Whichever approach you prefer, continue northwest from the intersection of the Alpine and Alpine Plateau Roads on a better surface to a small Forest Service guard station and turn south here (the only option). Pass the Big Blue Campground on the left and reach the trailhead just beyond (a total of 11.9 miles from CO 149, or 27.4 miles from U.S. 50). There is space for camping and for horse trailers at the trailhead, but the nearest sanitary facilities are located back down the road at Big Blue Campground.

Landmarks

- **0.0** Big Blue Trailhead.
- **0.3** Wilderness boundary.
- **1.5** Fall Creek enters valley from west.
- **4.2** First crossing of Big Blue Creek.
- **4.9** Rockslide area.
- **5.2** Slide Lake.
- **10.4** Big Blue Trailhead.

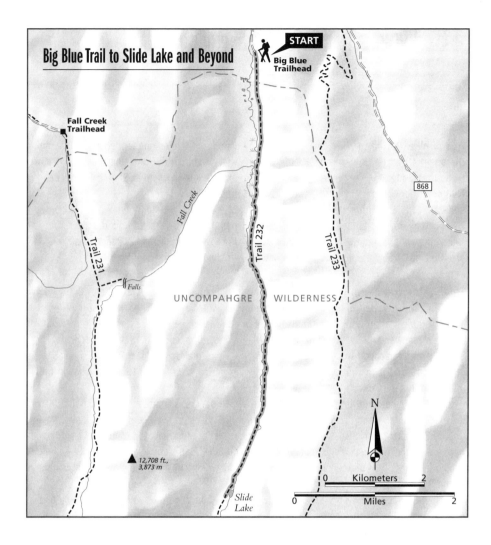

Big Blue Trail to Slide Lake and Beyond

START
Big Blue Trailhead

Fall Creek Trailhead

Fall Creek

868

Trail 231

Trail 232

Trail 233

UNCOMPAHGRE WILDERNESS

Falls

12,708 ft., 3,873 m

N

Slide Lake

0 Kilometers 2

0 Miles 2

The Hike

The Big Blue Trail follows a long, straight stream valley into the heart of the wilderness area near Uncompahgre Peak. While it is one of the more popular day hikes in the Uncompahgre, an overnight stay to enjoy the excellent fishing is also recommended. The trailhead, which lies just outside the wilderness boundary, is also a very popular fishing destination. The first 1.5 miles of the trail has only a few brief uphill sections as you pass through a picturesque large meadow formed by Big Blue Creek. The meadow narrows noticeably where Fall Creek drops into the valley from the southwest, but the trail remains flat and easy. At 3 to 4 miles from the trailhead, pass through several clearings with spectacular seasonal wildflower displays. A crossing of

Big Blue Creek at 4.2 miles could be tricky during the snowmelt season, but it was not difficult for us even after two days of off-and-on heavy rain.

Less than a mile beyond the crossing is the rockslide that has partially blocked Big Blue Creek to form Slide Lake. Here you will face a brief steep climb over rocky ground, though the payoff lies just beyond: Slide Lake is more than half filled in with sediment but is still an idyllic spot.

Options

There are many fine opportunities to include the Big Blue Trail as part of an extended hike into the deeper portions of the Uncompahgre Wilderness. One of these options is described (Hike 31) in detail in this book.

The Big Blue Trailhead.

17 Little Elk and Independence Trails

Forest Service Trails 244 and 234

Lush foothills terrain, wide variety of plant life, aspen groves, and a high level of solitude.

Type of hike: Day hike.

Distance: 12.1 miles point to point.

Difficulty: Difficult.

Trail conditions: Although this hike remains at relatively low elevation, never getting above 10,500 feet, there is enough elevation gain and loss to consider it a Difficult. Sections of the Little Elk Trail near the crossings of Elk Creek and Little Elk Creek can be very muddy. Substantial portions of the Little Elk Trail may be difficult to find, and it is recommended that you bring some map and compass skills

and a good sense of direction to the table for this hike. Neither trailhead is equipped with sanitary facilities. The Independence Trailhead is a poor option for trailhead camping, but the Little Elk North Trailhead along the Alpine Plateau Road does have limited space available.

Maps: USGS Alpine Plateau and Lake City 7.5-minute quadrangles.

Management: Gunnison Ranger District, Uncompahgre National Forest.

Finding the trailhead: The hike begins at the north end of the Little Elk Trail. Find the turnoff to the Alpine Road, on the west side of Colorado Highway 149, 11 miles north of Lake City or 33.6 miles south of the U.S. Highway 50/CO 149 intersection west of Gunnison. The Alpine Road is a bit rough and narrow but is passable for most passenger cars. The trailhead is well marked on the left, 3.1 miles from CO 149. You will also want to leave a shuttle vehicle at the end of the hike, at the Independence Trailhead. It is easy to spot on the west side of CO 149, 5.6 miles north of the intersection of Third Street and Gunnison in Lake City.

Landmarks

0.0 Little Elk North Trailhead.

1.8 Cross Elk Creek.

2.0 First crossing of Little Elk Creek.

3.9 Top of ridge above Little Elk Creek.

7.1 Cross High Bridge Gulch.

8.2 Cross Bill Hare Gulch.

9.5 Turn left onto Independence Trail.

11.0 Intersect waterline.

12.1 Independence Trailhead.

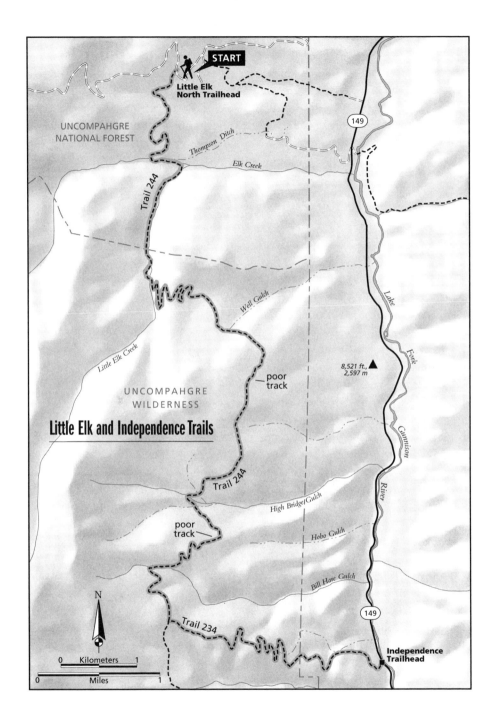

START

Little Elk
North Trailhead

UNCOMPAHGRE
NATIONAL FOREST

149

Thompson Ditch

Elk Creek

Trail 244

Well Gulch

Lake Fork

Little Elk Creek

8,521 ft.,
2,597 m

UNCOMPAHGRE
WILDERNESS

poor
track

Little Elk and Independence Trails

Trail 244

Gunnison

High Bridge Gulch

poor
track

Hobo Gulch

River

Bill Hare Gulch

N

149

Trail 234

Independence
Trailhead

0   Kilometers   1

0   Miles   1

The Hike

The Little Elk Trail traverses the northeastern foothills of the Uncompahgre Wilderness, parallel to the Lake Fork of the Gunnison River, at relatively low elevation. The terrain is mostly wooded, with plenty of water and a wide variety of plant life. This hike could instead be hiked from south to north, but in that direction it would involve considerably more elevation gain and route-finding difficulty. When I hiked this trail in the summer of 2001, some sections were obvious only because a horse party had passed through a few days earlier, refreshing the track somewhat. To avoid doing a large amount of off-trail wandering, be sure to bring (and know how to use) a map and compass, and follow this trail description as carefully as possible.

From the Little Elk Trailhead on the Alpine Road, begin hiking south, passing through a small grove of aspen trees. Hike downhill and parallel to a drainage for about 500 feet on a faint trail, then turn to the south not far above a fence line and irrigation ditch (shown on the USGS Alpine Plateau quadrangle as the Thompson Ditch No. 2). Climb briefly under tree cover, then meet the fence line and proceed south-southwest through a meadow. Follow a blunt ridge downhill for a few hundred yards, and drop off this to the northeast. The trail is well established as it descends numerous switchbacks, generally taking you in a southeast direction. As you approach Elk Creek, follow it back upstream and cross some logs. The trail then follows the south bank of Elk Creek back to the east and downstream for about 0.2 mile, and crosses Little Elk Creek at a muddy area.

Following the second creek crossing, pick up a trail heading southwest up the drainage of Little Elk Creek. This section of trail may be quite muddy, but in another 0.2 mile or so you will cross to the somewhat drier northwest side of the creek. For the next 1.2 miles, you will follow a good trail up the west side of Little Elk Creek, past the wilderness boundary. This section gains elevation steadily as it passes below a prominent 300-foot, west-facing cliff. The trail briefly crosses to the east side of the creek, then back to the west, and in another 0.2 mile you cross Little Elk Creek for the last time. If you are in need of water, fill your containers here; the next reliable water source is at High Bridge Gulch, more than 4 miles ahead.

In the next 0.7 mile, you will climb approximately 500 feet, one of two major uphill sections on this hike. Numerous switchbacks make the gradient of the climb reasonable, and at approximately 3.9 miles from the trailhead you reach the ridgetop. If you doubt your ability to follow a very faint trail, it might be best to turn around at this point. Follow the ridge back to the northeast for a few hundred feet before dropping east toward Well Gulch via switchbacks. The next section of trail may become quite obscure, and it is quite difficult to follow if you are reversing the hike to go from south to north. Still in Well Gulch, you will hike along the west, south-west, and south sides of a large meadow to a marker post. Pass through an area of large aspen to a smaller clearing and two more marker posts, then reenter the trees and follow a better trail uphill to the south-southeast. Continue steadily uphill to the

Aspen grove, Little Elk Trail.

south on a faint but passable track, emerging near the top of a large clearing that is visible on the USGS Alpine Plateau quadrangle (you are now at a point just over a mile west of the benchmark labeled "8521" near the Lake Fork of the Gunnison River). A marker post is installed here and will be critical should you need to reverse the trail back to the north.

Pass through the clearing and hike to the south through aspen to a second large clearing, exiting from the trees at a break in a fence line. Once again, remember this spot as a landmark in case you need to make a return trip. Angle slightly uphill across the second clearing, looking for a marker post at its south end. Turn a corner and cross an open hillside to the south-southwest into the last small drainage before High Bridge Gulch. Hike back south-southeast through the trees and turn the corner into High Bridge. A good track descends the north side of High Bridge Gulch, this time in a generally west-southwest direction. Drop through aspen trees for a short distance before crossing the creek itself, then climb back out of the drainage to the southeast.

On the south side of High Bridge Gulch, gain a blunt ridgeline that you follow on a faint trail almost directly to the east, then drop to the south through a stunningly beautiful stand of aspen and cross a small tributary drainage. A long, steady ascent to the southeast, bending gradually to the south, leads out of High Bridge Gulch. Follow the northwest edge of a meadow (the trail is again quite obscure) in the middle of this section. A little over 400 feet of elevation is gained before several switchbacks finally lead the way onto a ridgeline next to some rock outcrops. This ridge separates Bill Hare Gulch to the south from Hobo and High Bridge Gulches to the north. Cross an open, south-facing slope in a westerly direction, gradually descending into Bill Hare Gulch, then hike uphill and southeast after the creek crossing. Cross another minor ridgeline, descend across on open slope on its south side, and hike uphill through trees to the southeast after crossing another very small drainage. A section of flat to mild uphill grades leads south, dropping slightly and finally reaching the intersection of the Little Elk and Independence Trails. A sign indicates directions back to the north on the Little Elk, and also eastward to the Independence Trailhead (Trail 234).

Turn left (southeast) across an open hillside, ascending slightly, and pass through a gap in a small rock outcrop. Follow the trail downhill over open east- and southeast-facing hillsides, passing through many switchbacks and some small areas of tree cover. At about 1.5 miles from the Little Elk/Independence Trail junction, descend to a saddle at an elevation of approximately 9,400 feet. At this point a waterline (originating at a diversion some distance up Independence Gulch) releases its water into a small drainage that descends to the northeast. Hike downhill and parallel to this drainage, crossing it about 0.2 mile below the saddle, then pass to the southeast across an open hillside. A switchback leads back to the northeast just before you reach another saddle, then descend steeply to the east under tree cover. Cross a hillside of sage, juniper trees, and seasonal wildflowers to where the trail drops into a flatter area. Pass the wilderness boundary sign; a final very short but steep descent leads to the Independence Trailhead and CO 149.

18 Larson Lakes, Little Elk, and Independence Trails

Forest Service Trails 236, 244, and 234

A variety of wooded foothills terrain and an easy car shuttle.

Type of hike: Day hike.
Distance: 10.9 miles point to point.
Difficulty: Difficult.
Trail conditions: Portions of the Independence Trail can be difficult to find, so be confident about your map-reading skills before setting out. The two stream crossings should present no problem aside from possible wet feet. The Larson Lakes Trail lies outside the wilderness area, so you may encounter mountain bikes.
Maps: USGS Lake City 7.5-minute quadrangle.
Management: Gunnison Ranger District, Uncompahgre National Forest.

Finding the trailhead: The hike starts at the Crystal/Larson Trailhead on the northwest edge of Lake City. From Colorado Highway 149 find Balsam Drive, located approximately 0.9 mile north of the intersection of Third and Gunnison in Lake City. Drive west on Balsam Drive to a parking area just north of the cemetery. The trail starts as a steep dirt road just west of the parking area. Although you can drive the first 0.6 mile of the hike with a high-clearance four-wheel-drive vehicle, parking along the road is prohibited and there is little space for parking at the trailhead. From the lower parking area to the national forest boundary, please stay on the roadbed, as private land lies on either side. Neither trailhead has sanitary facilities nor space for camping. You will also want to leave a shuttle vehicle at the Independence Trailhead located on the west side of CO 149, 5.6 miles north of the intersection of Third Street and Gunnison in Lake City.

Landmarks

0.0 Crystal/Larson Trailhead.

0.6 Larson Lakes and Crystal Lake Trails split; turn right.

1.3 Unmarked trail to Thompson Lake; continue on the main trail.

4.1 Cross Larson Creek.

4.7 Signed trail to Larson Lakes; continue on the main trail.

5.2 Junction with Little Elk Trail; turn right.

7.4 Cross Independence Gulch.

8.2 Junction with Independence Trail; turn right.

9.8 Bottom of waterline.

10.9 Independence Trailhead.

The Hike

The Larson Lakes/Little Elk/Independence Trail linkup is one of the few in this book that stays below timberline for its entire length. As such, it requires somewhat

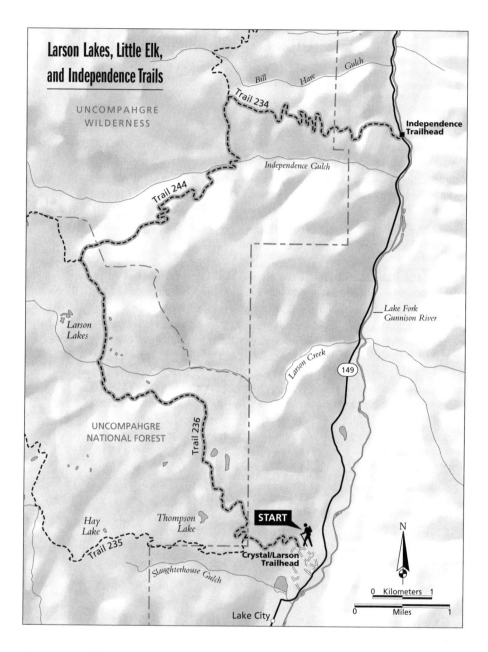

Larson Lakes, Little Elk, and Independence Trails

UNCOMPAHGRE
WILDERNESS

Bill *Hare* *Gulch*

Trail 234

Independence Trailhead

Independence Gulch

Trail 244

Larson Lakes

Lake Fork Gunnison River

Larson Creek

149

UNCOMPAHGRE
NATIONAL FOREST

Trail 236

START

Hay Lake

Thompson Lake

Trail 235

Crystal/Larson Trailhead

Slaughterhouse Gulch

N

0 Kilometers 1

0 Miles 1

Lake City

less exertion than many others. Still, its length and some stout uphill hiking will make for a full day.

Begin hiking steeply uphill to the west, following a roadbed for 0.6 mile to a gate. The Crystal Lake Trail (Trail 235) continues behind the gate, but instead take the well-marked Larson Lakes Trail (Trail 236) to the right. Proceed for approximately a mile to the north and northwest, mostly on contour with some short moderate uphill sections. At 1.3 miles an unsigned trail breaks left to Thompson Lake. At approximately 2 miles the trail turns to the northwest and then to the west as it enters the drainage of Larson Creek. The wide, flat trail crosses several small tributary streams, then crosses Larson Creek at 4.1 miles. Moderate uphill grades lead through a meadow to a signed trail intersection at 4.7 miles. The side trail leads a short distance to Larson Lakes, but you will stay on the main trail. About a half mile above the meadow, you will reach a flat saddle where the trail turns more to the west.

At the saddle a trail branches to the northeast; this is the Little Elk Trail (Trail 244), the next leg of the hike. About 500 feet down the Little Elk Trail from the junction is a wilderness boundary sign (here you are finally entering the Uncompahgre, though it's not obvious whether you are leaving or entering). From the boundary, a corridor through the trees leads north, then generally northeast down a steady grade. Bend more to the east as you enter the drainage of Independence Gulch, still steadily downhill. In places the track is faint, but it can be followed with the help of occasional tree blazes. Pass a short, steep downhill, a small clearing, and a switchback to a larger clearing where the track may disappear. Hike northeast past a marker post in the clearing, then bear slightly uphill and left past another post rather than continuing down the drainage. Tree blazes mark the way if you look carefully.

Beyond the clearing the trail begins to trend more to the north and downhill, and you will soon hear the sound of water. Hike parallel to the creek for a few hundred feet; good campsites with available water can be found in this area. At a switchback the trail crosses Independence Gulch. If necessary fill water containers here, as this is the last water source until you are within a mile of the Independence Trailhead. On the north side of the creek, it may be difficult to find the trail again, but look for an indistinct track heading northeast up a grassy hillside. Follow this for 300 to 400 feet and drop to the far (north) side of a small tributary drainage. Intersect a trail with a small sign indicating the direction back to the Larson Lakes Trail; if you are tired and looking for a way to shorten the hike, going right and downhill on this trail soon leads to a water diversion ditch and a relatively easy trip out to the Independence Trailhead. The more interesting route instead goes left and up a moderately steep grade on the narrow trail for approximately 0.2 mile to a clearing. Stay to the right (east or northeast) side of the clearing, following marker posts. Near the upper end of the clearing, pick up the trail as it reenters the trees. Pass through fantastic groves of mature aspen, hiking generally in a northerly direction. As you approach the ridgeline between Independence Gulch and Bill Hare Gulch, the Independence Trail (Trail 234) departs to the east, while the Little Elk Trail continues to the north into Bill Hare Gulch. The intersection is marked by a small sign indicating the Independence Trail.

From the junction with the Independence, proceed to the east across south-facing hillsides, then through a notch in a small ridge of rock. Descend across mostly

Cathy Crick on the Independence Trail.

open hillsides, through numerous switchbacks, in a generally east-southeast direction. At a flat spot you will intersect the waterline that diverts water from Independence Gulch not far from your last stream crossing. The waterline discharges into a small unnamed drainage that you will now follow for the next half mile or so. Descend the well-worn trail to the northeast and east, crossing the drainage at least once. Continue down hillsides of grasses, sage, and juniper trees, with one stretch of steep downhill gradient. Just above the trailhead you will pass the wilderness boundary sign, and a final short but very steep descent will deposit you at the Independence Trailhead and CO 149.

19 Larson Lakes and Crystal Lake Loop

Forest Service Trails 236 and 235

Diverse terrain on a loop hike with no car shuttle necessary.

Type of hike: Day hike or overnight.
Distance: 13.8-mile loop.
Difficulty: Difficult.
Trail conditions: The trail is easy to follow in its entirety. Almost 5 miles of the hike is located above timberline and therefore subject to the usual hazards, such as lightning and high winds. The Larson Lakes Trail is open to mountain bikes up to the wilderness boundary.
Maps: USGS Lake City 7.5-minute quadrangle; a very short section near the junction of the two trails is located on the USGS Uncompahgre Peak 7.5-minute quadrangle.
Management: Gunnison Ranger District, Uncompahgre National Forest.

Finding the trailhead: The hike starts and finishes at the Crystal/Larson Trailhead on the edge of Lake City. From Colorado Highway 149 find Balsam Drive, located approximately 0.9 mile north of the intersection of Third and Gunnison in Lake City. Drive west on Balsam Drive to a parking area just north of the cemetery. The trail starts as a steep dirt road just west of the parking area. Although you can drive the first 0.6 mile of the hike with a high-clearance four-wheel-drive vehicle, parking along the road is prohibited and there is very limited space for parking at the trailhead. From the lower parking area to the national forest boundary, please stay on the roadbed, as private land lies on either side. The trailhead has no sanitary facilities or space for camping.

Landmarks

0.0 Crystal/Larson Trailhead.
0.6 Larson Lakes and Crystal Lakes Trails split; turn right.
1.3 Unmarked trail to Thompson Lake; continue on the main trail.
4.1 Cross Larson Creek.
4.7 Trail to Larson Lakes; continue on the main trail.
5.2 Junction with Little Elk Trail; turn left (west).
7.4 Junction with Crystal Lakes Trail; turn left (south).
10.4 Crystal Lake.
11.8 Hay Lake.
13.2 Junction with Larson Lakes Trail.
13.8 Crystal/Larson Trailhead.

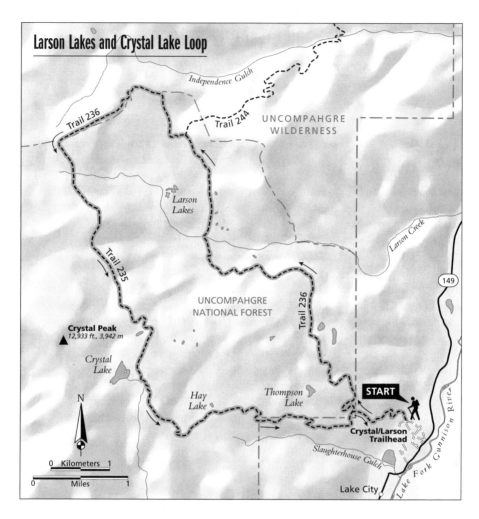

Larson Lakes and Crystal Lake Loop

Independence Gulch

Trail 236

Trail 244

UNCOMPAHGRE
WILDERNESS

Larson
Lakes

Larson Creek

Trail 235

149

UNCOMPAHGRE
NATIONAL FOREST

Trail 236

Crystal Peak
12,933 ft., 3,942 m

Crystal
Lake

N

Hay
Lake

Thompson
Lake

START

Crystal/Larson
Trailhead

Slaughterhouse Gulch

0 Kilometers 1

0 Miles 1

Lake City

Lake Fork Gunnison River

The Hike

The Larson Lakes (Trail 236) and Crystal Lake (Trail 235) Trails intersect not far from the northern reach of the Ridge Stock Driveway and can therefore be used as means of access to the central and western portions of the Uncompahgre Wilderness. Most of the traffic on these trails, however, appears to consist of day hikers enjoying either the loop hike or one of the trails individually. This loop may also be hiked in the opposite direction, starting with the Crystal Lake Trail. Either way it provides a strenuous and scenic outing. Commence hiking up the dirt road for approximately 0.6 mile past the cemetery to a very small gated parking area. The Larson Lakes Trail begins to the right (east) of the gate at the trailhead, while the Crystal Lake Trail takes off directly behind the gate. Follow the Larson Lakes Trail generally north on easy to moderate grades for the first mile or so. At 1.3 miles an unmarked trail departs to the left for Thompson Lake. At just over 2 miles from the trailhead, bend to the northwest and west into the drainage of Larson Creek, and at approximately 4.1 miles cross Larson Creek.

Beyond Larson Creek progress may slow, as the uphill grades increase. At the upper end of a large meadow is a signed trail that departs on the left to Larson Lakes, 0.3 mile distant. About a half mile above the meadow, the trail turns more to the west, and you reach a saddle. The Little Elk Trail (Trail 244) departs to the north from here, but you will continue on the Larson Lakes Trail. Beyond the trail junction and still below timberline, the Larson Lakes Trail begins to bend more to the west and west-southwest. From a ridgeline head southwest into trees, then at timberline switchback through a grassy area with rock outcrops. Another 100 feet of elevation gain will deposit you on a remarkably flat plateau that is nearly equal in size to the town of Lake City. If the weather is at all clear the way is obvious; follow marker posts for about 0.7 mile toward the mountainside to the west-southwest, and join the Crystal Lake Trail here.

The large plateau where Larson Lakes and Crystal Lake Trails meet.

To return to the Crystal/Larson Trailhead via the Crystal Lake Trail, proceed from the trail junction to the southeast and south on a good trail. Pass through the upper part of the Larson Creek drainage, and continue to contour to the south-southeast at approximately the 12,000-foot level. Drop into the trees below the steep northeast side of Crystal Peak, passing Crystal Lake to the west at a point approximately 3 miles from the Larson Lakes/Crystal Lake Trail junction. From the lake contour to the southeast, dropping off the ridgeline via switchbacks, and continue on a moderate descent through aspen to the east-northeast toward Hay Lake. From here descend through switchbacks into the drainage of Slaughterhouse Gulch and across an open slope with a fine view of Lake City below. Continue downhill to the east on a good trail, with a short section of contouring to the north before reaching the original gated trail junction once again. Follow the roadbed back downhill, past the cemetery, to the trailhead.

Options

From the junction of the Larson Lakes and Crystal Lake Trails, the central Uncompahgre Wilderness is accessible via the nearby Ridge Stock Driveway.

20 El Paso Creek Trail to Uncompahgre Peak

Forest Service Trails 238, 233, and 239

An uncrowded alternative route to the summit of a fourteener, with fine views to the high peaks of the Uncompahgre Wilderness.

Type of hike: Day hike.
Distance: 10.3-mile loop.
Difficulty: Difficult.
Trail conditions: Several sections of this trail may be difficult to follow, particularly just before and at the point where you will turn to the northwest into the drainage of El Paso

Creek. Once in the drainage, assuming decent visibility, the massive form of Uncompahgre Peak will be hard to miss.
Maps: USGS Uncompahgre Peak 7.5-minute quadrangle.
Management: Gunnison Ranger District, Uncompahgre National Forest.

Finding the trailhead: From the corner of Second and Gunnison in Lake City, go west on Second Street for two blocks. Turn left at the stop sign onto the Henson Creek Road (Hinsdale County Road 20). At 5.2 miles from Lake City is the well-marked Nellie Creek Road. This point is easily reached in a passenger car, but the very rough Nellie Creek Road requires a high-clearance four-wheel-drive vehicle. Hike, or if possible drive or catch a ride, approximately 3 miles to the lower end of a meadow on the left and across the creek, approximately a mile below the Uncompahgre Peak Trailhead. If you are driving, find a parking space a little farther up the road and look for some boards or logs on which to cross Nellie Creek. From the crossing head to the south end of the meadow, where the trail begins at the edge of the trees. A trailhead sign is visible from the road, but only if you look carefully. There are no sanitary facilities at the trailhead, but decent campsites are available in the area.

Landmarks

0.0 El Paso Trailhead.
0.9 Clearing at 11,800.
1.6 Wilderness boundary.
2.9 Crossing of El Paso Creek tributary.
4.6 Intersect southeast ridge of Uncompahgre Peak.
5.5 Uncompahgre Peak.
6.4 Intersect Uncompahgre Peak Trail; turn left (east).
8.4 Trail fork where Uncompahgre Peak Trail leaves the Ridge Stock Driveway; turn right (west).
9.3 Uncompahgre Peak Trailhead.
10.3 El Paso Trailhead.

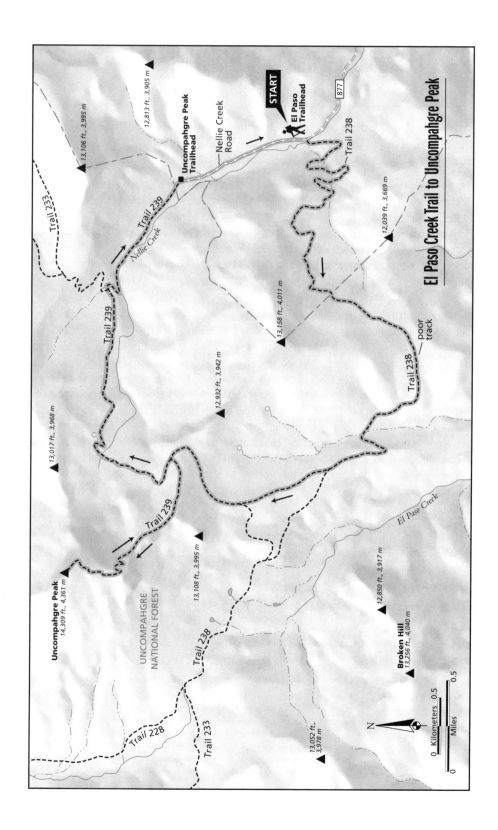

START

El Paso Trailhead

Nellie Creek Road

Uncompahgre Peak Trailhead

Nellie Creek

Trail 239

Trail 239

Trail 233

Trail 238

Trail 238

poor track

877

Trail 238

El Paso Creek

Trail 239

Trail 239

Uncompahgre Peak
14,309 ft., 4,361 m

UNCOMPAHGRE
NATIONAL FOREST

Trail 238

Trail 233

Trail 228

12,813 ft., 3,905 m

13,106 ft., 3,995 m

12,039 ft., 3,669 m

13,158 ft., 4,011 m

12,932 ft., 3,942 m

13,017 ft., 3,968 m

13,108 ft., 3,995 m

12,850 ft., 3,917 m

Broken Hill
13,256 ft., 4,040 m

13,052 ft.,
3,978 m

N

0 Kilometers 0.5

0 Miles 0.5

El Paso Creek Trail to Uncompahgre Peak

The Hike

This hike is a little-traveled alternative route to the summit of Uncompahgre Peak. It shares the last mile of the southeast ridge of Uncompahgre Peak with the much more crowded Uncompahgre Peak Trail, but until the ridge you may well have this hike to yourself.

The first mile of the El Paso Creek Trail (Trail 238) follows an old roadbed and wanders considerably more than is shown on the USGS quadrangle map. Mild grades, many switchbacks, and three crossings of a small tributary lead to a clearing at about 11,800 feet, below the jagged peak of Point 13,158. The roadbed bends to the northwest, then to the north up the east side of the clearing, reentering the trees. Resist the several informal side trails and stay on the wide roadbed. A short climb leads to a switchback, then to a long traverse southwest below the cliffs of Point 13,158.

You will pass the wilderness boundary sign and timberline at approximately 1.6 miles, and soon after will begin a nearly level traverse (the general direction is to the southwest) with fine views of the peaks to the south of Henson Creek. The track may disappear briefly but is easy to pick up again. As the trail begins to bend more to the west, a spectacular view of (left to right) Broken Hill, Wetterhorn Peak, Matterhorn Peak, and the mass of Uncompahgre Peak develops. Where the terrain begins to drop off more sharply to the west, follow a track that stays high and right, and turn toward the northwest into the drainage of El Paso Creek.

The next section of trail loses about 200 feet of elevation as it approaches a tributary (good water source) of El Paso Creek. Follow a switchback up the west side of the tributary, and where the trail meets a blunt ridgeline take a hard right. Follow the ridge to where it begins to widen. Instead of following the El Paso Creek Trail to the west of the ridgeline, follow the topographic high to the north–northwest. At an elevation of about 12,700 feet, you will meet an obvious right-angling trail (designated to be part of the Ridge Stock Driveway, Trail 233) that climbs northeast to the low point of Uncompahgre Peak's southeast ridge. From the southeast ridge simply follow the last mile of the Uncompahgre Peak Trail (Trail 239)—very likely with lots of company—to the broad summit of Uncompahgre. On the descent you can certainly reverse your course down the El Paso Creek Trail, but it is much easier to follow the well-traveled Uncompahgre Peak Trail to its trailhead; from here walk another mile down the Nellie Creek Road to your starting point.

Options

As the El Paso Creek Trail connects with other system trails to the south and southwest of Uncompahgre Peak, there are numerous ways to extend it to create multiday hikes to different trailheads. One of these is the hike out to the East Fork Trailhead described in this book as Hike 30. In addition, the El Paso Creek Trail can also connect to the Ridge Stock Driveway (Trail 233) to hike out to the Matterhorn or

Wetterhorn (left) and Matterhorn Peaks from El Paso Creek Trail.

Mary Alice Creek Trailheads, or even farther south to American Flats. To extend the hike in this manner, follow the blunt ridgeline described above only briefly, keeping an eye out for a faint trail that angles left (northwest), more or less on contour. Follow this toward and across the base of a prominent scree-covered hillside. Pass through some low hills, in a west-northwesterly direction, and over a low saddle or divide. A short but steep descent leads to a three-way trail intersection at the upper end of the East Fork of the Cimarron River. The trail that departs to the west from the intersection leads over Matterhorn Pass, a short downhill hike to the Matterhorn Trailhead.

21 Uncompahgre Peak Trail

Forest Service Trail 239

A popular peak (fourteener) climb, mostly above timberline.

Type of hike: Rigorous day hike.
Distance: 7.6 miles out-and-back (from Uncompahgre Peak Trailhead).
15.4 miles out-and-back (from base of Nellie Creek Road).
Difficulty: Moderate.
Trail conditions: This is by far the most crowded trail in the Uncompahgre Wilderness; you are encouraged to try one of the alterna-

tive routes to the summit, one of which is described in this book (Hike 20). Several other published descriptions of this trail are available, and this one is kept somewhat brief.
Maps: USGS Uncompahgre Peak 7.5-minute quadrangle.
Management: Gunnison Ranger District, Uncompahgre National Forest.

Finding the trailhead: The Uncompahgre Peak Trailhead is located on a four-wheel-drive road that follows Nellie Creek. From the corner of Second and Gunnison in Lake City, go west on Second Street for two blocks. Turn left at the stop sign onto the Henson Creek Road (Hinsdale County Road 20). At 5.2 miles from Lake City is the well-marked Nellie Creek Road. This point is easily reached in a passenger car, but the very rough and narrow Nellie Creek Road requires a high-clearance four-wheel-drive vehicle. Hike, or if possible drive or catch a ride, 3.9 miles to the end of the Nellie Creek Road and the trailhead. There are abundant campsites available along the Nellie Creek Road, and a handful of sites along the Henson Creek Road below. Public outhouses are available both at the base of the Nellie Creek Road and at the trailhead.

Landmarks

0.0 Base of Nellie Creek Road.

3.9 (0.0) Uncompahgre Peak Trailhead.

4.8 (0.9) Intersect the Ridge Stock Driveway; turn left (west).

6.8 (2.9) Intersect the southwest ridge of Uncompahgre Peak; turn right (west).

7.7 (3.8) Uncompahgre Peak.

11.5 (7.6) Uncompahgre Peak Trailhead.

15.4 Base of Nellie Creek Road.

The Hike

Uncompahgre Peak (14,309 feet) is a graceful and shapely "fourteener" located near the center of the Uncompahgre Wilderness Area. It is the highest peak in the San Juan Mountains, and despite its fearsome appearance has two very hikeable trails to its summit. If you own or rent a four-wheel-drive high-clearance vehicle, or if you can catch a ride up the Nellie Creek Road, the ascent of Uncompahgre is a relatively easy

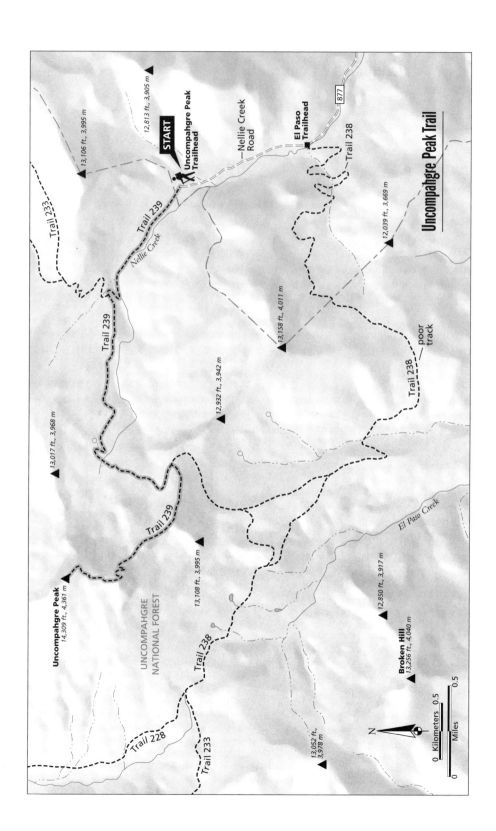

Uncompahgre Peak Trail

12,813 ft., 3,905 m

13,106 ft., 3,995 m

START

Uncompahgre Peak Trailhead

Nellie Creek Road

El Paso Trailhead

877

Trail 238

12,039 ft., 3,669 m

Trail 233

Trail 239

Nellie Creek

Trail 239

13,158 ft., 4,011 m

13,017 ft., 3,968 m

12,932 ft., 3,942 m

poor track

Trail 238

Trail 239

El Paso Creek

Uncompahgre Peak
14,309 ft., 4,361 m

13,108 ft., 3,995 m

UNCOMPAHGRE
NATIONAL FOREST

Trail 238

12,850 ft., 3,917 m

Broken Hill
13,256 ft., 4,040 m

Trail 228

13,052 ft.,
3,978 m

Trail 233

N

0 Kilometers 0.5

0 Miles 0.5

Uncompahgre Peak from near Matterhorn Pass.

day for a fourteener; otherwise plan on a very long but spectacular day-hike or back-packing outing.

Begin driving (or, if absolutely necessary, hiking) up the Nellie Creek Road. There are two crossings of Nellie Creek, as well as a couple of sections on the upper part of the road where vehicles frequently get stuck. The trailhead is located at approximately 11,500 feet, 3.9 miles from the Henson Creek Road. Follow the now youthful Nellie Creek for approximately 0.8 mile, where a switchback right leads to a signed junction with the Big Blue Trail. Don't take the switchback, but rather head west toward Uncompahgre Peak, following a well-worn trail. Continue through a broad valley and up onto the southeast ridge at an elevation of about 12,900 feet. Simply proceed up this ridge to the huge summit area.

Options

The intersection with the Ridge Stock Driveway at 0.9 mile leads to many possibil-ities for extended, overnight hikes. The options include connections to the Little Cimarron Trail (Trail 229), the Fall Creek Trail (Trail 231) the Big Blue Trail (Trail 232, Hike 31), and, via the Ridge Stock Driveway, any of the trails that traverse the Uncompahgre to the northwest of Lake City.

22 Matterhorn Peak

Forest Service Trail 233

A peak hike with arguably the best summit view in the Uncompahgre.

Type of hike: Day hike.
Distance: 6.4 miles out-and-back.
Difficulty: Moderate.
Trail conditions: The trail is generally dry, with no stream crossings. The portion that climbs the southeast slopes of Matterhorn Peak does not follow an established track, but the way is abundantly clear.
Maps: USGS Uncompahgre Peak 7.5-minute quadrangle.
Management: Gunnison Ranger District, Uncompahgre National Forest.

Finding the trailhead: From the corner of Second and Gunnison in Lake City, zero your odometer and go west on Second Street for two blocks. Turn left at the stop sign onto the Henson Creek Road (County Road 20). Proceed on this road for 9.1 miles to the Capitol City townsite, and turn right onto the North Henson Creek Road. North Henson is rough but passable for most passenger cars. Two miles up this road, the high-clearance four-wheel-drive Matterhorn Creek Road heads north 0.6 mile to the trailhead. A rocky area at 1.3 miles on the North Henson Creek Road will stop some passenger cars; from here it is an easy half-mile walk to the Matterhorn Creek Road. No sanitary facilities are available at the trailhead. Dispersed campsites are abundant both at the trailhead and along the North Henson Creek Road.

Landmarks

0.0 Matterhorn Trailhead.
0.7 Junction with Trail 245 (Matterhorn Cutoff).
1.2 Wilderness boundary.
1.5 Intersect the trail connecting with the Matterhorn Cutoff; turn right (north).
2.6 Matterhorn Pass.
3.2 Matterhorn Peak.
6.4 Matterhorn Trailhead.

The Hike

From the Matterhorn Trailhead pleasant hiking up a roadbed for 0.7 mile leads to a clearing where the trail takes a pair of switchbacks uphill and to the right (northeast). Resume a steady grade to the north–northwest toward Wetterhorn Peak, which now dominates the skyline. Reenter the trees at about 11,460 feet and pass the wilderness boundary sign. Continue to tree line at 1.3 miles and a detailed view of the peak ahead.

    The trail continues on a steady grade up the east side of the basin, with the upcoming hike up the south slopes of Matterhorn becoming increasingly clear. Head up a steeper, crumbly section of trail on a low ridge between two drainages to

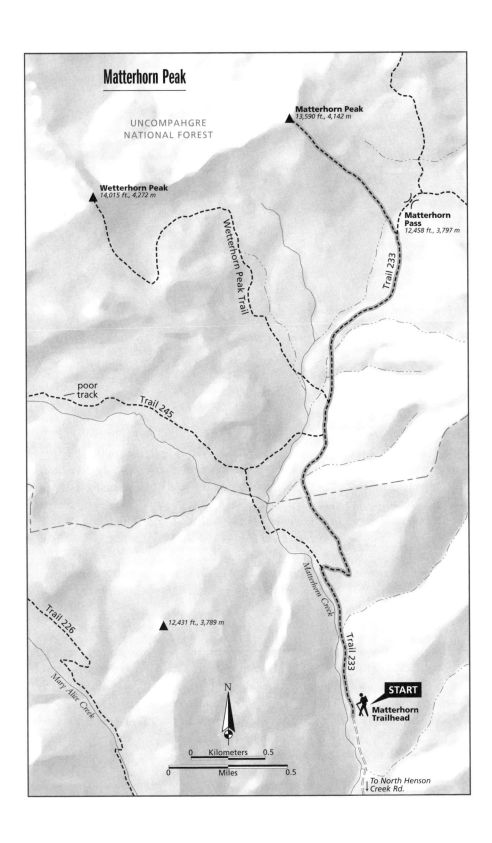

Matterhorn Peak

UNCOMPAHGRE
NATIONAL FOREST

Matterhorn Peak
13,590 ft., 4,142 m

Wetterhorn Peak
14,015 ft., 4,272 m

Matterhorn Pass
12,458 ft., 3,797 m

Wetterhorn Peak Trail

Trail 233

poor track

Trail 245

Trail 226

12,431 ft., 3,789 m

Mary Alice Creek

Matterhorn Creek

Trail 233

START

Matterhorn Trailhead

N

Kilometers 0.5
0

Miles 0.5
0

To North Henson Creek Rd.

West from the Matterhorn Creek Trail.

where the grade decreases and the trail bends to the north. The last half mile to Matterhorn Pass (the informal name given to the 12,458-foot saddle southeast of Matterhorn's summit) presents much easier hiking on a good trail with a mild grade. You can depart for the south slopes at any point along this stretch. Continuing to the pass before starting up Matterhorn will save perhaps 100 to 200 feet of elevation gain, but the overall distance covered will be correspondingly longer. Either way, the south slopes present easy walking on grass to a level of about 13,000 feet before giving way to steep but stable talus. From the summit all of the major peaks of the Uncompahgre Wilderness are visible, including Wetterhorn to the southwest, Coxcomb, Redcliff, and Precipice Peak to the northwest, Silver Mountain to the northeast, and the massive bulk of Uncompahgre to the east.

Options

The high saddle to the southeast of Matterhorn Peak (here referred to as Matterhorn Pass) is a fine jumping-off point to more distant parts of the Uncompahgre Wilderness. A multiday hike from the Matterhorn Trailhead over Matterhorn Pass and north into the East Fork of the Cimarron River (via the East Fork Trail, Trail 228) is only one possibility. The climb to Uncompahgre Peak from the Matterhorn Trailhead via Matterhorn Pass and the upper El Paso Creek Trail is a popular alternative route up Uncompahgre.

23 Wetterhorn Peak

Forest Service Trail 233

A spectacular and exposed fourteener climb.

Type of hike: Day hike.
Distance: 7 miles out-and-back.
Difficulty: Difficult.
Trail conditions: Mostly clear and dry trail. Some exposed scrambling is required on the summit pitch. Some may prefer to use a rope on this part, and it is recommended that you not climb below others here.
Maps: USGS Uncompahgre Peak and Wetterhorn Peak 7.5-minute quadrangles.
Management: Gunnison Ranger District, Uncompahgre National Forest.

Finding the trailhead: From the corner of Second and Gunnison in Lake City, zero your odometer and go west on Second Street for two blocks. Turn left at the stop sign onto the Henson Creek Road (Hinsdale County Road 20). Proceed up Henson Creek for 9.1 miles, and turn right onto the North Henson Creek Road. This road is a bit rough but passable for most passenger cars. Two miles up North Henson Creek Road, the high-clearance four-wheel-drive Matterhorn Creek Road heads north (right) 0.6 mile to the trailhead. A rocky area at 1.3 miles on the North Henson Creek Road will stop some passenger cars; from here it is an easy half-mile walk to the Matterhorn Creek Road. No rest room facilities are available at the trailhead, but nice informal campsites are abundant.

Landmarks

   0.0 Matterhorn Trailhead.
   0.7 Junction with Trail 245 (Matterhorn Cutoff).
   1.2 Wilderness boundary.
   2.7 Intersect southeast ridge of Wetterhorn.
   3.5 Wetterhorn summit.
   7.0 Matterhorn Trailhead.

The Hike

Wetterhorn Peak is an elegant and challenging member of the fourteeners club. Perhaps due to a short section of exposed scrambling just below the summit, it seems to receive much less traffic than does its sibling Uncompahgre Peak. Wetterhorn is remarkably difficult to view without considerable hiking; it is visible but not obvious from the highway north of Montrose. While Uncompahgre is easily visible from both U.S. Highways 50 and 550, to view Wetterhorn from the car you will have to drive almost all the way to Engineer Pass. Wetterhorn is a memorable and highly recommended peak climb. As with the hike up Uncompahgre, the trail is described well in several "fourteeners" books; therefore this description is kept brief.

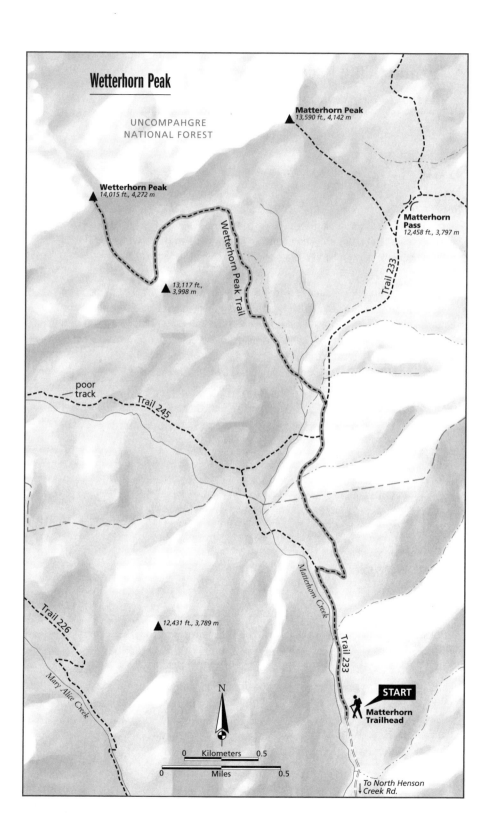

Wetterhorn Peak

UNCOMPAHGRE
NATIONAL FOREST

Matterhorn Peak
13,590 ft., 4,142 m

Wetterhorn Peak
14,015 ft., 4,272 m

**Matterhorn
Pass**
12,458 ft., 3,797 m

Wetterhorn Peak Trail

Trail 233

13,117 ft.,
3,998 m

poor
track

Trail 245

Matterhorn Creek

Trail 226

12,431 ft., 3,789 m

Trail 233

Mary Alice Creek

START

**Matterhorn
Trailhead**

N

0   Kilometers   0.5

0   Miles   0.5

To North Henson
Creek Rd.

Wetterhorn Peak.

From the Matterhorn Trailhead pleasant hiking up a roadbed for 0.7 mile leads to a clearing where the trail takes a pair of uphill switchbacks to the right. After the second switchback resume a steady grade to the north-northwest toward Wetterhorn Peak, now dominating the western skyline. Reenter the trees at about 11,460 feet and pass the wilderness boundary sign. At 1.3 miles from the trailhead, you reach tree line and the first clear view of Matterhorn Peak. Continue until the trail turns to the north along the east side of the valley.

The best point to leave the main trail toward Wetterhorn is not obvious, but it may be near where the drainage to the west splits into two. On the west side of the drainage, pick up a track that climbs steadily up the west side of the valley. At about 12,800 feet turn briefly to the south to gain the notch between Point 13,117 and the main peak of Wetterhorn. Follow the ridge via some scrambling to a notch below the summit block, which is climbed via ledgy, fourth-class rock to the summit. A rope may be appreciated for this last section by those not accustomed to exposed scrambling. The view from the summit of Wetterhorn is unparalleled, taking in all of the high peaks of the Uncompahgre Wilderness, as well as the chaotic terrain of Cow Creek beyond Wetterhorn Basin to the west.

24 Matterhorn Cutoff to Wetterhorn Basin Overlook

Forest Service Trails 233 and 245

A high degree of solitude (after a half mile) and intimate views of Wetterhorn Peak.

Type of hike: Day hike.
Distance: 6.4 miles out-and-back.
Difficulty: Moderate.
Trail conditions: For some distance in the upper Matterhorn Creek drainage, there is no good track to follow—but there is also little opportunity to get lost. On many days you will have this hike to yourself once you leave the

Wetterhorn Peak Trail. The destination for this hike is referred to here as the Wetterhorn Basin Overlook, but this is not an official or recognized name.
Maps: USGS Uncompahgre Peak and Wetterhorn Peak 7.5-minute quadrangles.
Management: Gunnison Ranger District, Uncompahgre National Forest.

Finding the trailhead: From the corner of Second and Gunnison in Lake City, zero your odometer and go west on Second Street for two blocks. Turn left at the stop sign onto the Henson Creek Road (Hinsdale County Road 20) and drive 9.1 miles to the Capitol City townsite. Turn right onto the North Henson Creek Road, which is rough but passable for most passenger cars. Two miles up this road, the high-clearance four-wheel-drive Matterhorn Creek Road heads north 0.6 mile to the trailhead. A rocky area at 1.3 miles on the North Henson Creek Road will stop some passenger cars; from here it is an easy half-mile walk to the Matterhorn Creek Road. There are several good campsites along the North Henson Creek Road, and also along the first half mile of the Matterhorn Creek Road. No sanitary facilities are available at the trailhead.

Landmarks

0.0 Matterhorn Trailhead.
0.7 Leave the Matterhorn Creek Trail.
0.9 First creek crossing.
1.1 Second creek crossing.
2.5 Turn north on trail to overlook.
3.2 Wetterhorn Basin Overlook.
6.4 Matterhorn Trailhead.

The Hike

This uncrowded day hike leads to a 13,100-foot saddle on the ridge that descends to the west from Wetterhorn Peak. From the saddle an unimpaired view of the monolithic west face of Wetterhorn, as well as of the slightly lower peaks to the north of Wetterhorn Basin, gives all the incentive necessary to fight the steady uphill grade out of the valley of Matterhorn Creek.

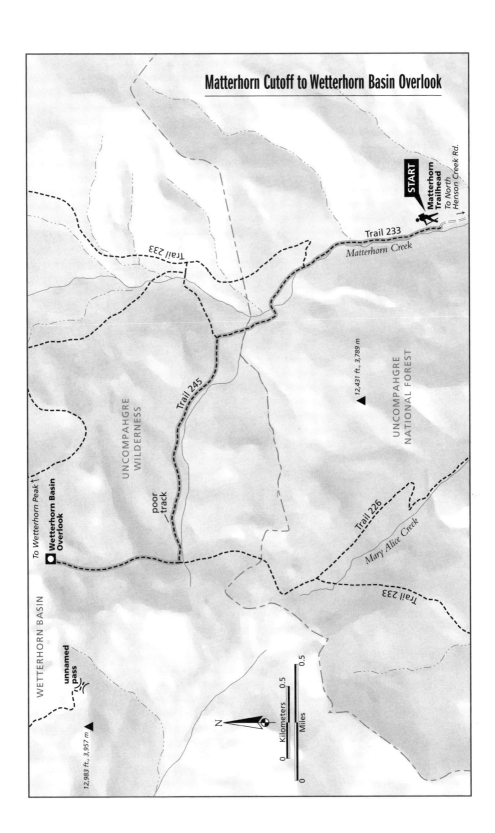

Matterhorn Cutoff to Wetterhorn Basin Overlook

START
Matterhorn
Trailhead

To North
Henson Creek Rd.

Trail 233

Matterhorn Creek

Trail 233

Trail 245

12,431 ft., 3,789 m

UNCOMPAHGRE
NATIONAL FOREST

UNCOMPAHGRE
WILDERNESS

poor
track

To Wetterhorn Peak

Wetterhorn Basin
Overlook

Trail 226

Mary Alice Creek

Trail 233

WETTERHORN BASIN

unnamed
pass

12,983 ft., 3,957 m

N

Kilometers   0.5

Miles   0.5

0

0

From the gated Matterhorn Trailhead, begin hiking moderately and steadily uphill, with a fine view of Wetterhorn Peak appearing at about a half mile. Turn onto the Matterhorn Cutoff (Trail 245), to the left and unsigned, just as the main trail begins a major uphill switchback to the right (east). Follow the east side of a small meadow, crossing to the west side of Matterhorn Creek at the meadow's uphill end. The trail is not at all obvious as it reenters the trees, but you should be able to find it directly west of the crossing. The trail climbs through the trees, soon flattens out again as it passes through an often wet area, and crosses to the north side of the creek. Head uphill along the northeast side of a meadow where the track may become faint, then traverse west-southwest along the base of a steeper barren slope. A short trail departs to the east from here, connecting to the main Matterhorn Creek Trail 0.4 mile to the northeast. For your return trip note where these two trails meet, as the right turn down the hill to the Matterhorn Trailhead is easy to miss.

Wetterhorn Peak from the Matterhorn Cutoff.

The next three-quarters of a mile of hiking parallels Matterhorn Creek on its north or northeast side; a track may appear now and then, but you will be mostly improvising. Take the easiest line while staying within approximately 200 feet of the creek. Climb up onto a rocky knoll and continue hiking to the west and upstream. At the upper end of the valley, connect with the obvious trail, which rises toward a low area on the ridgeline to the north; a rather arduous and steady climb of about 500 feet leads to a small basin and, soon thereafter, to the Wetterhorn Basin Overlook. The view from the overlook to the northeast is dominated by the west face of Wetterhorn Peak, and to the north by Coxcomb and Redcliff.

Return via the same route you followed on the way up. As previously described, it may be easy to miss the right turn, near timberline, back to the Matterhorn Trailhead. It is located at the east side of a prominent area of willows. If you do miss it, simply proceed about 0.4 mile to the east and northeast to link up with Trail 233 south of Matterhorn Peak. Head south, down the prominent switchbacks of the Matterhorn Creek Trail, to the trailhead. It is also not difficult to hike out via the Mary Alice Creek Trail (Trail 226), described in this book under Hike 25. If you did not leave a vehicle along the North Henson Creek Road at the base of the Matterhorn Road, this will force you to hike 0.6 mile up the Matterhorn Road to retrieve your vehicle.

Options

A natural and logical extension of this hike leads from the head of Matterhorn Creek south toward Mary Alice Creek and the southern end of the Ridge Stock Driveway. Hike 25 describes a loop beginning at the Mary Alice Creek Trailhead that includes most of this hike in the reverse direction.

25 Mary Alice Creek and Matterhorn Cutoff to Matterhorn Trailhead

Forest Service Trails 226 and 245

An uncrowded hike with fine views of the remote and rugged Cow Creek area.

Type of hike: Day hike.
Distance: 4.7 miles point to point.
Difficulty: Easy.
Trail conditions: The trail is easy to follow for the first 1.2 miles or so, after which it is likely to be faint. Once in the upper basin, simply staying near the east bank of Mary Alice Creek will keep you from getting lost.
Maps: USGS Wetterhorn Peak and Uncompahgre Peak 7.5-minute quadrangles.
Management: Gunnison Ranger District, Uncompahgre National Forest.

Finding the trailhead: From the corner of Second and Gunnison in Lake City, zero your odometer and go west on Second Street for two blocks. Turn left at the stop sign onto the Henson Creek Road (Hinsdale County Road 20) and drive 9.1 miles to the Capitol City townsite. Turn right onto the North Henson Creek Road, which is rough but passable for most passenger cars. At 2.8 miles from the Henson Creek Road, a rough, unmarked road heads right (north) a short distance to the trailhead. While there are no sanitary facilities at the trailhead, informal campsites are abundant along the North Henson Creek Road.

You may also wish to leave a vehicle at the Matterhorn Trailhead or at the base of the Matterhorn Road (the Matterhorn Road requires a high-clearance four-wheel-drive vehicle). The road begins 2 miles from the Henson Creek/North Henson Creek intersection, and 0.8 mile below the turnoff to the Mary Alice Creek Trailhead. The Matterhorn Trailhead is located a very rough 0.6 mile up the Matterhorn Road.

Landmarks

0.0 Mary Alice Creek Trailhead

0.5 Crossing of Mary Alice Creek.

1.8 Junction with Ridge Stock Driveway; turn right.

2.1 Cow Creek overlook.

2.4 Saddle and wilderness boundary sign.

2.6 Intersect Trail 245; turn right (east).

4.0 Intersect Matterhorn Creek Trail; turn right (south).

4.7 Matterhorn Trailhead.

The Hike

This is a seldom-traveled route that can be used as a relatively easy approach to the southern portion of the Ridge Stock Driveway, but it also presents a worthy day hike

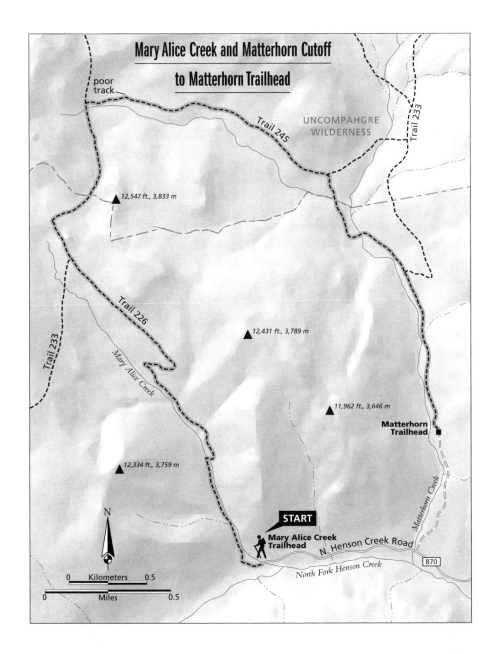

Mary Alice Creek and Matterhorn Cutoff to Matterhorn Trailhead

poor track

Trail 245

UNCOMPAHGRE WILDERNESS

Trail 233

▲ 12,547 ft., 3,833 m

Trail 226

Trail 233

Mary Alice Creek

▲ 12,431 ft., 3,789 m

▲ 11,962 ft., 3,646 m

Matterhorn Trailhead ■

▲ 12,334 ft., 3,759 m

N

START

Mary Alice Creek Trailhead

N. Henson Creek Road

Matterhorn Creek

870

North Fork Henson Creek

0   Kilometers   0.5

0   Miles   0.5

on its own. Count on a high level of solitude and fine high-country scenery on this hike. From the Mary Alice Creek Trailhead, begin hiking up a steep trail (Trail 226) that follows the west side of Mary Alice Creek. The grade is unrelenting for the first half mile, at which point the trail crosses to the east side of the creek and climbs through two switchbacks. Continue up the east side of the creek to tree line, where two more switchbacks help you maintain a northwesterly course. If you lose the trail, simply hike up the grassy slopes below a prominent southwest-facing cliff, parallel to the creekbed below. The obvious track descending from the southwest is the southern portion of the Ridge Stock Driveway, but this hike continues uphill and to the northwest to a saddle on the ridgeline above. From here a fine view of the chaotic Cow Creek basin to the west and northwest presents itself.

There are two tempting possible extensions to this hike, but neither is recommended. You may note a track that descends northwest into Middle Canyon; this appears to be used for moving grazing animals. There are no known trails that allow easy escape from the area, which consists of deeply dissected and cliffy volcanic beds. If you descend this trail, the best way out by far is to retrace your steps to the saddle. Also note that the trail shown on the Trails Illustrated map, heading north from

West from Cow Creek overlook, Mary Alice Creek Trail.

Cow Creek overlook and connecting into the Wetterhorn Basin Trail, simply does not exist. Because of extremely crumbly scree and steep hillside traverses, this route is not recommended.

To complete this hike to the Matterhorn Trailhead, descend back to the east-southeast, staying just below the steeper hillsides above. Hike into the 12,460-foot saddle just to the west of Point 12,547, shown on the Wetterhorn Peak quadrangle. From the saddle find a small wilderness boundary sign and descend north into a trough of sorts. In less than a half mile, you will reach the uppermost end of Matterhorn Creek. Follow the north side of the creek downstream for about three-quarters of a mile, with only an occasionally recognizable track, then pick up a better trail as the terrain steepens. Just beyond (east of) an area of willows, a split in the trail is easy to miss; the left fork heads east-northeast toward Matterhorn Peak, while you will take the right fork downhill and to the south, toward the Matterhorn Trailhead.

Cross a rocky dry drainage to a creek crossing, pass through a wet area, then contour for a bit and drop down a short grade. Just beyond is a small meadow and second crossing. On the east side of Matterhorn Creek, proceed a few hundred feet to the southeast and meet up with the old roadbed that constitutes the Matterhorn Creek Trail. Continue downhill and to the south on this for 0.7 mile to the Matterhorn Trailhead and, if your shuttle vehicle was left at the base of the Matterhorn Creek Road, for another 0.6 mile to the North Henson Creek Road.

Options

Mary Alice Creek is well situated to serve as the start of longer hikes in either direction along the Ridge Stock Driveway (Trail 233).

26 Engineer Pass to American Flats and Wildhorse Peak

Views of the Uncompahgre high peaks.

Type of hike: Easy half-day (or less) hike.
Distance: 6 miles out-and-back.
Difficulty: Easy.
Trail conditions: Engineer Pass is a well-known destination for four-wheel-drive and all-terrain vehicle enthusiasts, so there is a fair amount of traffic and noise in the area. Despite this, camping near the trailhead is

possible if weather permits. The entire length of this hike is subject to high wind and lightning during summer thunderstorms.
Maps: USGS Wetterhorn Peak and Handies Peak 7.5-minute quadrangles.
Management: U.S. Bureau of Land Management and USDA Forest Service.

Finding the trailhead: From the corner of Second Street and Gunnison in Lake City, go west two blocks and turn left at a stop sign. Proceed up the Henson Creek Road for 9.1 miles to the junction where the North Henson Creek Road turns right. Bear left here and continue up the valley of Henson Creek. All cars should be able to make it to the turnoff to Rose Cabin at 14.4 miles; from here hike or drive up the road that turns off to the right. Most passenger cars will make it to Thoreau Cabin at approximately 16 miles from Lake City; a sign recommends four-wheel-drive vehicles on the remainder of the road, but in dry conditions a passenger car can make it farther. If you are driving a high-clearance four-wheel-drive vehicle, proceed all the way to Engineer Pass, a total of 18 miles from Lake City.

Landmarks

0.0 Engineer Pass.
2.0 Intersection of Horsethief Trail (Trail 215) and the Ridge Stock Driveway (Trail 233).
3.0 Wildhorse Peak.
6.0 Engineer Pass.

The Hike

The majority of this hike is located in the area of American Flats, which is managed by the U.S. Department of the Interior, Bureau of Land Management, rather than the Forest Service. It is an amazing area of wide-open alpine tundra at which several major trails converge (the Bear Creek, Ridge Stock Driveway, and Horsethief Trails). Wildhorse Peak is the dramatic peak that lies to the north of American Flats. Wildhorse is prohibitively rocky and steep on all but the south and southeast sides, which provide a spectacular and reasonably easy peak hike.

From Engineer Pass hike northeast on a roadbed, which quickly narrows to a faint, gently descending trail. After a few hundred yards, take an option that breaks left and slightly uphill; the idea is to stay high and close to the mountainside to the

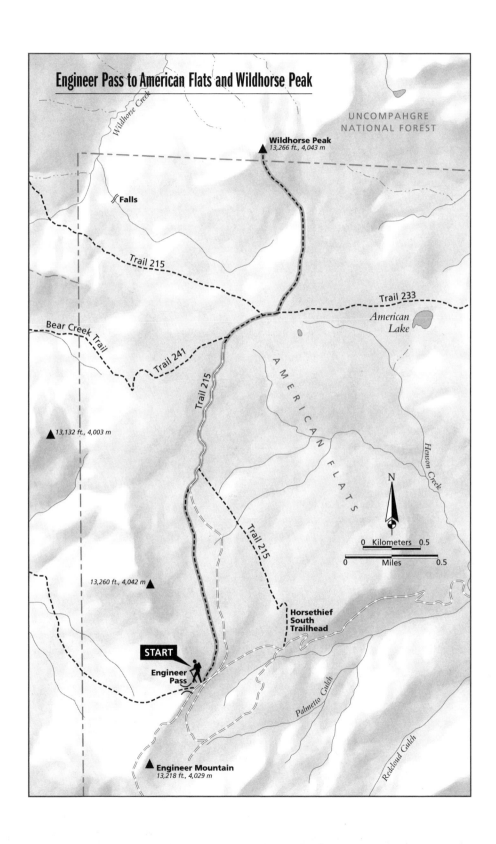

Engineer Pass to American Flats and Wildhorse Peak

Wildhorse Creek

UNCOMPAHGRE
NATIONAL FOREST

▲ Wildhorse Peak
13,266 ft., 4,043 m

Falls

Trail 215

Trail 233

American
Lake

Bear Creek Trail

Trail 241

Trail 215

A M E R I C A N   F L A T S

Henson Creek

▲ 13,132 ft., 4,003 m

N

0   Kilometers   0.5

0   Miles   0.5

13,260 ft., 4,042 m ▲

Trail 215

Horsethief
South
Trailhead

START

Engineer
Pass

Palmetto Gulch

Redcloud Gulch

▲ Engineer Mountain
13,218 ft., 4,029 m

west. The trail soon becomes a roadbed leading into the heart of American Flats, with wonderful views of (left to right) Wildhorse Peak, Coxcomb, Wetterhorn Peak, and Uncompahgre Peak. The trail becomes faint once again at about a half mile, as switchbacks belonging to the north spur of the Bear Creek Trail come into view to the northwest. Continue north, cross a small tributary stream, then trend more to the northwest. A couple of marker posts are in place here, but there is no real established track. Straight to the north is a long, low talus and scree slope with a decent trail along its base. Following this feature eventually leads to the signed three-way intersection of the Engineer Pass, Bear Creek, and Horsethief Trails with the Ridge Stock Driveway.

The route up Wildhorse Peak is obvious: From the trail junction hike northeast and uphill onto a narrowing ridgeline that descends southeast from the summit. From an elevation of about 12,600 feet, simply climb the grassy south slopes of Wildhorse to a short stretch of talus below the 13,266-foot summit. To complete this day hike, follow your tracks back to Engineer Pass.

In addition to the trail beginning at Engineer Pass, there is a quieter alternative approach for this hike. The official south end of the Horsethief Trail leaves the Engineer Pass Road about 1.4 miles above Thoreau Cabin and 0.6 mile below Engineer Pass. This trail climbs moderately at first, follows the base of a scree-covered hillside, and drifts mostly without an established track to the north-northeast to the aforementioned trail junction. The Horsethief Trail continues to the northwest from American Flats and proceeds over spectacular terrain to end up in the Dexter Creek drainage north of Ouray (see Hike 27).

Options

From the intersection of the Ridge Stock Driveway (Forest Service Trail 233) and the Bear Creek and Horsethief (Trail 215) Trails, substantially downhill hikes into the Ouray area (via either of the latter two trails) are possible for those who have made car shuttle arrangements.

◀ *Bill Crick in front of Wildhorse Peak.* Photo: Dan Hippe

Backpacks

27 Bear Creek National Recreation Trail to American Flats and Horsethief Trail

Forest Service Trails 241 and 215

Very diverse terrain including deep canyons, spruce-fir forests, high ridges, alpine tundra, and the Bridge of Heaven, all facilitated by a relatively simple car shuttle.

Type of hike: Two- to three-day backpack.
Distance: 15.5 miles point to point.
Difficulty: Difficult.
Trail conditions: The Bear Creek National Recreation Trail has several sections that are narrow and potentially exposed to rockfall. Move quickly through these sections, and be particularly aware during wet and windy weather. The transition from American Flats onto the northbound Horsethief Trail can be confusing, although recent (summer 2000)
trail work has clarified the route considerably. Be careful not to descend too far into either the Wildhorse Creek or Difficulty Creek drainages, as there are no established trails leading out from these areas. At least 7 miles of this hike lie above timberline and are subject to high winds and lightning.
Maps: USGS Ouray, Ironton, Handies Peak, and Wetterhorn Peak 7.5-minute quadrangles.
Management: Ouray Ranger District, Uncompahgre National Forest.

Finding the trailhead: From the southernmost intersection on the main street of Ouray, drive south on U.S. Highway 550 for 2.3 miles to the trailhead, located just south of a tunnel. Parking is available on both sides of the road. No sanitary facilities are present at the trailhead, and there is no space available for camping. Nearby campsites are located at the U.S. Forest Service Amphitheater Campground, just south of Ouray; informal sites can be found 6 to 8 miles farther south on U.S. 550. A shuttle vehicle should be left at the north end of the Horsethief Trail. To reach this trailhead, drive north 1.6 miles from the Ouray Hot Springs pool on U.S. 550. Turn right and drive up the Dexter Creek Road (Forest Road 871/Country Road 14) for 2.5 miles to the well-marked Dexter Creek Trailhead, where the road switchbacks right, across the creek. The trailhead is easily reached by passenger cars. Although camping is possible at the trailhead, it is a mediocre site and is not recommended. If you have a high-clearance four-wheel-drive vehicle, to 1.2 miles farther up the road to the well-marked Horsethief Trailhead.

Landmarks

0.0 Bear Creek National Recreation Trailhead.

2.5 Tributary crossing.

3.6 Yellowjacket Mine.

5.7 Saddle leading into American Flats.

6.3 Junction with Horsethief Trail.

8.0 Saddle between Wildhorse and Difficulty Creeks.

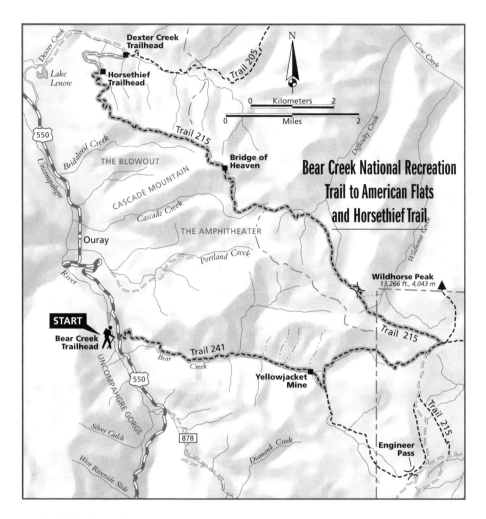

11.3 Bridge of Heaven.
15.5 Dexter Creek Trailhead.

The Hike

This hike presents an incredible variety of high-country terrain. Begin hiking south of the tunnel, on the west side of U.S. 550, 2.3 miles south of Ouray. As the trail leaves the highway, it crosses above the tunnel and tackles the very steep mountainside above. Numerous switchbacks armored with slate bedrock enable the fit hiker to gain elevation rapidly, and the highway noise will fade away. The last switchback is located at the base of a steep cliff of volcanic rock. Cross the top of the slate scree slope and continue across a ledge heading uphill and south. As the trail begins to turn the corner into the drainage of Bear Creek at about 0.9 mile, Red Mountain to the south and the Sneffels Range to the west come progressively into view.

Columbine along Horsethief Trail. Photo: Dan Hippe

The next half mile is fairly level and passes under several 300-foot-high cliffs. These portions of the trail are potentially subject to rockfall, particularly in wet or windy weather, so move quickly through these sections. An interesting attraction are exposures of the famous "giant ripples" of Ignacio Quartzite; these can be seen on the north-facing cliffs across Bear Creek. For perhaps a half mile, the trail follows ledges 200 feet or so above the creek, with some very steep drops below. Drop down and right across a tributary drainage at approximately 2.5 miles from the trailhead. Proceed from the tributary crossing east toward Bear Creek, where good campsites with water are available (remember to obey the trail and water camping buffer guidelines). Follow steeper grades on a very pleasant trail along the north side of Bear Creek. The remains of the Yellowjacket Mine are reached at about 3.6 miles; campsites and water supplies are abundant in the area of the mine.

From the Yellowjacket Mine hike south-southeast on a well-marked trail into the southern of the two drainages that come together in the area of the mine. In only a few minutes, you will reach a trail junction with a sign indicating the direction and distance back to U.S. 550. From the junction cut left onto a trail heading north and northeast up a steady grade. Follow this to an easy stream crossing. On the north side of the creek, follow what appears to be an old roadbed for about 0.3 mile into the upper basin above tree line. If you lose the trail, try to trend northeast, then east, without losing elevation, until it becomes obvious again. Continue generally east through the flower-filled tundra basin toward the obvious low point (also the wilderness area boundary) on the ridge ahead. From the high saddle, follow switch-backs downhill into American Flats. Cairns and marker posts lead east-northeast to a signed trail junction of the Bear Creek Trail, the Horsethief Trail (Trail 215), and the Ridge Stock Driveway (Trail 233).

From the trail intersection the track is not obvious, but a cairn is visible to the west-northwest. Pass this feature, losing elevation slightly but staying south of Wildhorse Creek. The trail becomes more distinct (this portion of the Horsethief Trail was improved considerably during the summer of 2000) as it passes through a wet area and turns more to the west. Cairns mark the way past another faint section of trail, and you will soon begin climbing toward the 12,650-foot pass located on the ridge to the northwest. Cross a couple of small drainages then continue uphill past cairns, past a couple of switchbacks, and through a notch between rock outcrops. A few more minutes of climbing leads to the pass, the high point of this hike. The pass presents a three-star view of the Sneffels Range to the west, Redcliff and Coxcomb to the northeast, and Wildhorse Peak, Wetterhorn Peak, and the tip of Uncompahgre Peak to the east. There may be large herds of elk along this ridge and to the northwest in the drainage of Difficulty Creek; hike quietly and you may be rewarded with the opportunity to view them.

The next section of trail descends steeply (approximately 650 feet in the next mile) to the north-northwest, into the upper drainage of Difficulty Creek. After crossing the creek, the trail begins to bend gradually to the west, with only minor uphill and downhill grades, before climbing west into the drainage of Cascade Creek. As the creekbed bends to the south, the trail maintains its westerly course for 0.2 mile to a pass at the head of Cascade Creek. From here begin descending next to the creek, which will probably be dry except during the snowmelt season. About a half mile west of the pass, the trail bends to the north and contours through a wooded area. Cross another small drainage and begin a series of steep switchbacks on the 400-foot climb to Bridge of Heaven. Just above the last switchback, the trail meets the ridgeline of Cascade Mountain. The view from the Bridge takes in Grand Mesa and the West Elk Mountains in the distance to the north and northeast, Dunsinane Mountain, Precipice Peak, Redcliff, and Coxcomb to the northeast, Red Mountains No. 1 and 2 to the south, and the Sneffels Range to the west.

From the Bridge of Heaven, the remainder of the hike is downhill. Drop briefly onto the ridge of Cascade Mountain, then follow switchbacks to the west and around the uppermost end of the Bridalveil Creek drainage. For a distance of almost 2 miles, the trail descends mostly on the south side of the ridge, heading in a west-northwest direction. At a point 1.9 miles from the Horsethief Trailhead is a saddle overlooking part of Ouray; from here break to the north (do not take the dead-end trail that heads west onto a rocky knoll) and follow switchbacks through a clearing and into the trees. Continue through the spruce forest on an excellent trail, coming finally upon either the Horsethief Trailhead or Dexter Creek Trailhead and your shuttle vehicle.

28 Middle Fork and East Fork Trails

Forest Service Trails 227 and 228

Alpine scenery unparalleled in the Uncompahgre.

Type of hike: Two- to three-day backpack.
Distance: 15.1 miles point to point.
Difficulty: Moderate.
Trail conditions: The Middle Fork Trail is extremely well maintained, and in normal conditions will be dry and easy to follow. The trail appears to receive relatively heavy use, but is still far from crowded. At least 4 miles of the trail lies above timberline and is therefore subject to the typical weather dangers, including high wind and lightning. There is no good track leading downhill from Middle Fork Pass into the East Fork of the Cimarron, but the terrain is not particularly difficult. Map-reading ability and a good sense of direction will be helpful on this portion of the hike. The East Fork Trail is generally easy to follow but has muddy portions where small drainages and (in wetter weather) debris flows cross the trail. Excellent, sheltered campsites with water are available near timberline in both the Middle Fork and East Fork drainages.
Maps: USGS Courthouse Mountain, Wetterhorn Peak, Uncompahgre Peak, and Sheep Mountain 7.5-minute quadrangles.
Management: Ouray Ranger District, Uncompahgre National Forest.

Finding the trailhead: This hike will involve a car shuttle between the Middle Fork and East Fork Trailheads. The Middle Fork Trailhead is located up a bumpy road from its intersection with the West Fork and East Fork Roads, about 2 miles above Silver Jack Reservoir. To reach this point from Montrose and points east, turn south from U.S. 50 toward Silver Jack Reservoir from a point 21.6 miles east of the U.S. 50/U.S. 550 intersection in Montrose and 2.6 miles east of Cimarron. Follow this road 19.5 miles, past the national forest boundary and Big Cimarron campground, and turn right toward Owl Creek Pass (a left turn heads to the East Fork Trailhead). At another 0.1 mile turn left onto the Middle Fork Road. From this last turn it is 4.7 bumpy miles to the trailhead. The same point can be reached from near Ridgway by taking the Owl Creek Pass Road (Ouray County Road 10), located 24.1 miles south of the U.S. 50/U.S. 550 intersection (Main Street and Townsend Avenue) in Montrose and 1.7 miles north of the traffic light in Ridgway. Follow this excellent gravel road for 15 miles over Owl Creek Pass, and turn left at the next intersection. The Middle Fork Road is well marked as it departs to the right approximately 6 miles beyond.

Most passenger cars should be able to negotiate the Middle Fork Road. Be aware, however, that the road is quite rocky, and that during wet weather it is not uncommon for small mudslides and debris flows to block the road in several places; having a high-clearance four-wheel-drive vehicle along will provide some insurance against being stuck until the road is cleared. The trailhead area has plenty of room for dispersed camping, but has no sanitary facilities. The area receives fairly heavy use, so please try to minimize your impact if camping here.

To leave a shuttle vehicle at the East Fork Trailhead, take the aforementioned left turn, which is well marked, onto the East Fork Road. Follow this (easily passable by passenger cars) for approximately 1.8 miles to the trailhead. The trailhead area has plenty of space for dispersed camping, and sanitary facilities are present.

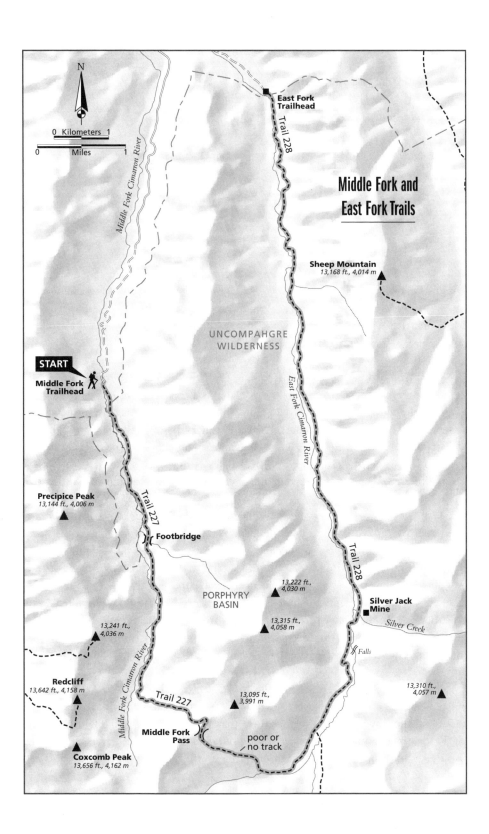

N

0 Kilometers 1

0 Miles 1

Middle Fork Cimarron River

East Fork Trailhead

Trail 228

Middle Fork and
East Fork Trails

Sheep Mountain
13,168 ft., 4,014 m

UNCOMPAHGRE
WILDERNESS

START
Middle Fork
Trailhead

East Fork Cimarron River

Precipice Peak
13,144 ft., 4,006 m

Trail 227

Footbridge

Trail 228

PORPHYRY
BASIN

13,222 ft.,
4,030 m

13,315 ft.,
4,058 m

Silver Jack
Mine

Silver Creek

13,241 ft.,
4,036 m

Middle Fork Cimarron River

Redcliff
13,642 ft., 4,158 m

Trail 227

13,095 ft.,
3,991 m

Falls

13,310 ft.,
4,057 m

Middle Fork
Pass

poor or
no track

Coxcomb Peak
13,656 ft., 4,162 m

Landmarks

0.0   Middle Fork Trailhead.

0.25 Wilderness boundary.

2.2   Footbridge over Porphyry Creek.

4.1   Sharp turn to southeast.

5.6   Middle Fork Pass.

6.3   Junction with East Fork Trail.

8.6   Silver Jack Mine.

15.1 East Fork Trailhead.

The Hike

A well-maintained and relatively easy trail (Trail 227) leads up the east side of the Middle Fork of the Cimarron River into a high meadow filled with dramatic mountain views and a wonderful variety of wildflowers. The descent into the East Fork of the Cimarron River involves cross-country hiking with little or no trail to follow, while the East Fork Trail (Trail 228) makes for a pleasant final day back to your shuttle vehicle.

The first 1.5 miles or so up the Middle Fork Trail is a veritable "freeway," with few loose or muddy sections to slow you down. Near the 2-mile point, the trail steepens and climbs in the trees to a point well above the creek. At just over 2 miles, a good-sized tributary creek descends from Porphyry Basin to the east; a rough trail departs for the basin from here. Cross the tributary and climb rather steeply out its south side, through switchbacks, to where it levels out once again. Pass through a couple of areas of heavy timber fall and a very nice, cruisy section of trail for 0.8 mile.

At about 3.5 miles from the trailhead, you enter the high meadow that makes up the upper part of the Middle Fork drainage and is the visual highlight of the hike. Wonderful views of Coxcomb, Redcliff, and various unnamed peaks compete with a stunning variety of wildflowers for your attention. After a narrow stretch of trail just above the river is an apparent split in the track; the slightly higher course presents a more obvious trail, but the two come back together in a few hundred yards in either case. In the upper part of the meadow, the trail remains well above (east of) the creek. Pass through some pockets of tree cover (good campsites) and begin climbing more steeply just before the eastward turn that characterizes the upper part of this hike.

After turning to the east and uphill, an excellent trail leads into the flower-filled upper basin. The trail fades near the 12,000-foot contour, but well-spaced marker posts lead the way (in foggy weather these may be difficult to find). The final climb of 300 feet is negotiated by way of a long switchback. From Middle Fork Pass the view takes in (from east-southeast through the south and west) Uncompahgre Peak,

East Fork of the Cimarron River. Photo: Dan Hippe

the saddle where the East Fork and El Paso Creek Trails join, Matterhorn Peak (connected to Wetterhorn via a jagged ridge), Wetterhorn Peak, Point 13,411 just above
the pass, Coxcomb, Redcliff, Point 13,241, Precipice Peak, and Dunsinane Mountain.

From Middle Fork Pass it will be necessary to hike cross-country (but fortu-
nately downhill), with little or no established trail to follow, for approximately 1.3
miles into the East Fork drainage. Hike in the general direction of an area of greenish
rock outcrops in the near distance. As the terrain steepens you will want to bear
more to the east near the 12,300-foot level. At a point almost directly north of Matterhorn Peak's summit, it is best to drop steeply to the south to avoid the cliff- and
talus-strewn mountainsides that drop eastward toward the East Fork. Near the creek
bear east and downstream, eventually picking up a track that bends to the northwest,
into the drainage of the East Fork of the Cimarron River.

A mile-long stretch of trail descends gently along a bench, eventually dropping
more steeply toward the creek near the first areas of tree cover. A sign here indicates

where the East Fork Trail departs across the river to climb south toward the high saddle between Matterhorn and Uncompahgre Peaks. Continue to the north-northeast (downstream) through interspersed meadows and tree cover; the trail becomes faint in one area but is easy to pick up again. Just before crossing a tributary creek, you reach an area that obviously receives heavy camping use; remember to camp at least 100 feet off the trail if you wish to settle in this area for the night. Once across the tributary make rapid progress to the north and cross the East Fork at a point just above the Silver Jack Mine. The staining of the creekbed in the upper East Fork appears to have originated in a mineralized area of rock at the base of the north and northeast shoulder of Matterhorn Peak, not from sources related to mining. Remains of the Silver Jack Mine include a couple of collapsed buildings and small amounts of mining equipment. This area appears to have been devastated by an avalanche, probably originating high on the west side of the river and spreading its destruction well up onto the east side. Continue north through this area, passing a meadow and heading back into the trees (decent campsites are available near here). Below is a stretch where fallen timber and water on the trail may slow progress; large avalanche chutes descend down the opposite (west side) mountain walls. At about 10,300 feet the trail passes onto the Sheep Mountain quadrangle map.

Continue north on a good track; at one point the trail narrows and diverts around an area of heavy fallen timber, but in general there are few obstacles for the next 2 miles. In numerous locations small mudflows have crossed the trail, cutting dramatic channels down the hillside and at times depositing some of their cargo in the level areas where they cross the trail. At one point perhaps 2.5 miles from the East Fork Trailhead a tributary drainage is crossed, and at just under a mile from the trailhead is an attractive meadow, but in general the final 3 miles simply proceed down the east side of the East Fork of the Cimarron. The East Fork Trailhead and your shuttle vehicle are likely to be a welcome sight.

29 Fall Creek and Little Cimarron Trails

Forest Service Trails 231 and 229

A fine, diverse high-country hike that requires only a 5-mile car shuttle.

Type of hike: Two- to three-day backpack.
Distance: 15.6 miles point to point.
Difficulty: Moderate.
Trail conditions: See below.
Maps: USGS Sheep Mountain and Uncom-
pahgre Peak 7.5-minute quadrangles.
Management: USDA Forest Service. The Fall Creek portion is managed by Gunnison Ranger District, the Little Cimarron portion by Ouray Ranger District.

Finding the trailhead: From U.S. Highway 50, turn south onto a dirt road signed LITTLE CIMARRON ROAD. The turnoff is located 41.1 miles west of the intersection of U.S. 50 and Colorado Highway 135 in Gunnison and 22.9 miles east of the intersection of U.S. 50 and U.S. 550 in Montrose. Follow the Little Cimarron Road (a little rough in places but easily passable by passenger cars) for 15.6 miles to a small road that cuts down and right. This is the Little Cimarron Trailhead, which presents the best trailhead camping in the area and is a possible endpoint for this hike. It is suggested instead (whether you are camping at Little Cimarron or not) that you leave a vehicle 0.4 mile farther up the Little Cimarron Road at a hairpin turn that constitutes the Little Cimarron East Trailhead. This trailhead will make the end of the hike a bit shorter and much easier.

To locate the second trailhead and the start of the hike, continue past the hairpin for just over 4 more miles (a total of 20.1 miles from U.S. 50) to the Fall Creek Trailhead on the right. There is plentiful parking here, including space for horse trailers. Trailhead camping at Fall Creek is possible, but the previously described Little Cimarron Trailhead is much better suited.

Trail conditions: A few sections on the lower Fall Creek Trail are likely to be wet and boggy. You will have to negotiate a total of four stream crossings, two in the Fall Creek drainage and two more in the Little Cimarron drainage. Only the lower Little Cimarron crossing, which can be avoided if necessary by continuing down the main Little Cimarron Trail, is likely to be difficult or dangerous if river flows are high. This entire hike takes place on mostly well-established trails, although there are a few short sections without a good track.

Both trails can receive heavy packhorse traffic. Campsites with available water are abundant except for the 4-mile stretch where you will cross the high ridge dividing the two drainages. The ridge also should be avoided if thunderstorms are approaching, as it is very exposed to the elements (although quick exits off the ridgetop are available). The ridge reaches an elevation of more than 12,800 feet, therefore this hike requires a good degree of fitness.

The areas near timberline in both the Fall Creek and Little Cimarron drainages are recommended for campsites. This allows crossing of the high ridge between Fall Creek and the Little Cimarron River early on the second day, and serves to split the hike into three days of approximately equal time and effort. Finding your way off the ridgetop on the Little Cimarron Trail is tricky. Either familiarity with the location or solid map-reading skills will be helpful.

The junction of the Fall Creek and Little Cimarron Trails can lead to extended hikes into the central part of the Uncompahgre via the upper portion of the Fall Creek Trail. Once over the

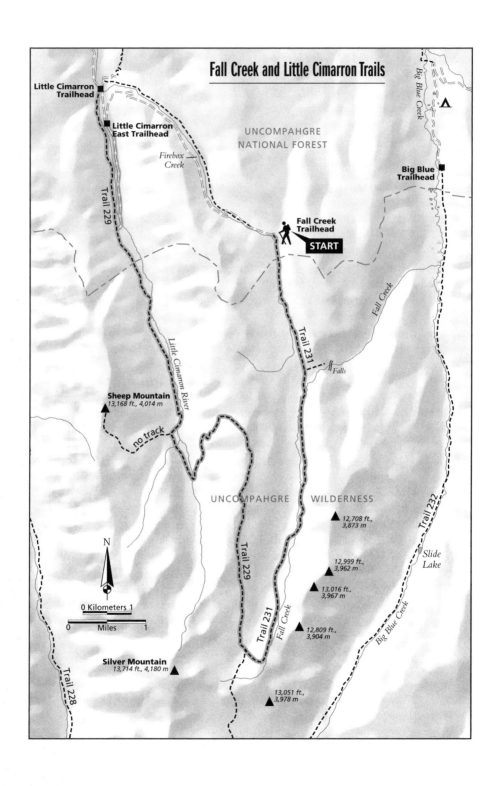

Fall Creek and Little Cimarron Trails

Little Cimarron Trailhead

Little Cimarron East Trailhead

Firebox Creek

UNCOMPAHGRE NATIONAL FOREST

Big Blue Creek

Big Blue Trailhead

Trail 229

Fall Creek Trailhead

START

Trail 231

Little Cimarron River

Fall Creek

Falls

Sheep Mountain
13,168 ft., 4,014 m

no track

N

UNCOMPAHGRE WILDERNESS

12,708 ft., 3,873 m

12,999 ft., 3,962 m

Trail 232

Slide Lake

Trail 229

13,016 ft., 3,967 m

0 Kilometers 1

0 Miles 1

Trail 231

Fall Creek

12,809 ft., 3,904 m

Big Blue Creek

Trail 228

Silver Mountain
13,714 ft., 4,180 m

13,051 ft., 3,978 m

divide at the south end of the Fall Creek drainage, connect up with the Big Blue Trail (Trail 232) or the Ridge Stock Driveway (Trail 233).

Landmarks

0.0 Fall Creek Trailhead.

1.8 Firebox Creek/Fall Creek divide.

2.1 First crossing of Fall Creek.

3.9 Second crossing of Fall Creek.

6.0 Junction of Fall Creek and Little Cimarron Trails; turn right (north).

9.2 Timberline descending Little Cimarron Trail.

10.5 Upper crossing of Little Cimarron River.

14.0 Junction with Little Cimarron East Trail; turn right.

15.6 Little Cimarron East Trailhead.

The Hike

The loop hike connecting the Fall Creek (Trail 231) and Little Cimarron (Trail 229) Trails is a compelling overnight hike that begins with open high meadows, passes over a high-alpine ridge on a good trail, and finishes with deep subalpine spruce-fir forests. The loop has the added attraction of requiring only a very easy 5-mile car shuttle between the two trailheads. The Fall Creek Trail starts at an elevation of approximately 11,000 feet, thereby giving relatively easy access to the central high country of the Uncompahgre Wilderness. Although there is enough climbing to feel like you've done some work on the hike, the final 9 miles are either flat or downhill. The hike's total distance means that a very fit hiker could possibly complete it in a day; most will require at least two. A more leisurely three-day period works best for finding sheltered campsites with water sources, as you cross the high ridge on the second day. Hiking this route in two days will involve either one long day and one short, or camping high on the exposed ridge that divides the two drainages.

Leave a vehicle at the Little Cimarron East Trailhead and begin hiking from the Fall Creek Trailhead. Start briefly downhill from the southwest side of the trailhead parking area. You reach the wilderness boundary almost immediately as the trail enters a meadow along Firebox Creek. Climb briefly up a low hill, with a short downhill stretch behind it, and enter a beautiful, wide meadow. The flat and easy trail continues up the east side of the meadow to another brief climb and subsequent descent. Here you will pass into the drainage of Fall Creek, which bends to the east near this point, passes over a waterfall, and descends northeast into Big Blue Creek. Take the trail straight south to the first stream crossing at 2.1 miles.

For the next 1.5 miles, the trail simply follows the east side of a huge, beautiful meadow. It may become boggy and difficult to follow in a few spots. Although well below tree line, this meadow is exposed and should be avoided during thunderstorms.

Scenery along the Little Cimarron Trail.

The meadow gradually narrows, and you soon reach the second crossing of Fall Creek at 3.9 miles. On the far (west) side of the crossing, the trail begins to climb mildly but steadily, and you may notice several campsite possibilities. The track becomes faint in one grassy section but is obvious where it reenters the trees. The next section of trail, near the south border of the Sheep Mountain quadrangle map, climbs steadily under tree cover and is likely to be muddy. This section also passes through several avalanche runout zones, which could make for difficult or even dangerous hiking conditions during the early part of the season.

The last major stand of trees features possible sheltered campsites but not a lot of level ground. Above tree line, in an open flowered meadow, the trail loses about 150 feet of elevation, but it soon regains its steady uphill course. Several small tributary drainages provide water here if needed. Above is a small flat area with the remains of a wooden structure. At times during the summer, this area serves as a high camp for sheepherders; be prepared to encounter sheep and/or people in the area. From the flat area the trail becomes indistinct; head to the south-southwest for a few hundred feet to pick up a more obvious track that soon angles back uphill to the northwest. The intersection with the Little Cimarron Trail (Trail 229) is approximately at the toe (lowest point) of the large scree field below the craggy peak to the west. Beyond the trail junction you will face by far the most difficult portion of this hike as you angle steeply uphill to the northwest on the Little Cimarron Trail. The grade eases briefly, then gains about 300 feet on one last climb to the ridgetop. Once on the ridge the track is fairly obvious as it heads directly north, briefly reaching an elevation above 12,800 feet. You should make good time on almost 2 miles of slightly downhill hiking along the ridge, leading to a broad saddle at an elevation of approximately 12,250 feet.

The track that descends into the Little Cimarron drainage from the area of the saddle may be sketchy, but look for it directly to the west from the saddle's low point. Find a better trail angling to the northwest into one of the highest areas of tree cover. As the trail turns more to the west-southwest, it passes through a meadow with a marker post; find the trail reentering the woods near the meadow's southwest corner. Cruise downhill parallel to a drainage on the north, then more to the south and southwest for 0.7 mile. The trail continues to lose elevation rapidly through this section. You will soon come upon the higher of two crossings of the Little Cimarron River. With relatively little water this high in the drainage, the crossing should not present a problem. On the west side of the Little Cimarron is a large meadow that makes a compelling camping area. Spectacular views of the sunrise on the slopes of Silver Mountain are the main reward for spending the night here. The area also provides tree cover, a reliable water source, and a straightforward 5-mile hike to finish out the next day. Remember to camp well away from the trail, and preferably in the trees, to be out of sight from the trail.

For the last leg of the journey to the Little Cimarron East Trailhead, hike north-northwest on a good trail, pass into the trees, and cross a small drainage. Descend briefly to the northeast, then turn to the north just above the creek to a small clearing (possible campsite). Turn downhill and past another small drainage, then resume a northerly course through alternating clearings (these are actually enormous winter and springtime avalanche runout zones) and wooded areas. Five clearings are passed in the next 1.5 miles, during which you will lose about 500 feet of elevation. Below is a mile or so of hiking mostly under tree cover; keep an eye out for a fairly obvious spur trail that departs from the main trail to the right and downhill. Follow this for about a quarter mile to the final crossing of the Little Cimarron River.

This crossing could potentially be dangerous in high runoff conditions, but we had little trouble with it even after two days of heavy rain. If you don't like the looks of it, simply retrace your steps to the main Little Cimarron Trail and continue north on it for about 1.8 miles to the footbridge at the Little Cimarron Trailhead. If you left a vehicle at the Little Cimarron East Trailhead (at the hairpin), leave your pack and hike 0.4 mile up the Little Cimarron Road to retrieve it. If you do manage the lower crossing, all that is left is about 1.4 miles on one of the easiest sections of trail in the Uncompahgre. This section is an old roadbed, and it will feel like a freeway.

30 El Paso Creek and East Fork Trails

Forest Service Trails 238 and 228

Cross a divide among the highest peaks in the Uncompahgre.

Type of hike: Two- to three-day backpack.
Distance: 15.2 miles point to point.
Difficulty: Moderate.
Trail conditions: Parts of the El Paso Creek Trail may be grown over but are not difficult to find. Two crossings of the East Fork of the Cimarron River are necessary, but neither is difficult.
Maps: USGS Uncompahgre Peak and Sheep Mountain 7.5-minute quadrangles.
Management: Gunnison and Ouray Ranger Districts, Uncompahgre National Forest.

Finding the trailhead: To reach the El Paso Trailhead and the start of the hike, drive west for two blocks from the corner of Second and Gunnison in Lake City. Turn left at the stop sign onto the Henson Creek Road (Hinsdale County Road 20). At 5.2 miles from Lake City is the well-marked Nellie Creek Road. This point is easily reached in a passenger car, but the Nellie Creek Road requires a high-clearance four-wheel-drive vehicle. Hike, drive, or catch a ride approximately 3 miles to the lower end of a meadow on the far (west) side of Nellie Creek. If you are driving, find a parking space a little farther up the road and look for some boards or logs on which to cross the creek. This point is located approximately a mile below the Uncompahgre Peak Trailhead. From the crossing head to the south end of the meadow, where the trail begins at the edge of the trees. A trailhead sign is visible from the road if you look carefully. There are no amenities at the trailhead, but good campsites are available in the area.

You will also want to leave a shuttle car at the East Fork Trailhead, a remarkably long driving distance from the starting point of the hike. To reach the East Fork Trailhead from Montrose and points east, turn south from U.S. Highway 50 toward Silver Jack Reservoir from a point 21.6 miles east of the U.S. 50/U.S. 550 intersection in Montrose and 2.6 miles east of Cimarron. Follow this road 19.5 miles, past the national forest boundary and Big Cimarron campground, and trend left onto the East Fork Road. Follow this (easily passable by passenger cars) for approximately 1.8 miles to the trailhead. The trailhead area has plenty of space for dispersed camping, and sanitary facilities are present.

Landmarks

   0.0 El Paso Trailhead.

   0.9 Clearing at 11,880 feet.

   1.6 Wilderness boundary.

   2.9 Crossing of El Paso Creek tributary.

   5.0 Junction with East Fork Trail; turn right (north).

   6.0 Cross to west side of the East Fork Cimarron River.

   8.6 Cross Silver Creek.

  15.2 East Fork Trailhead.

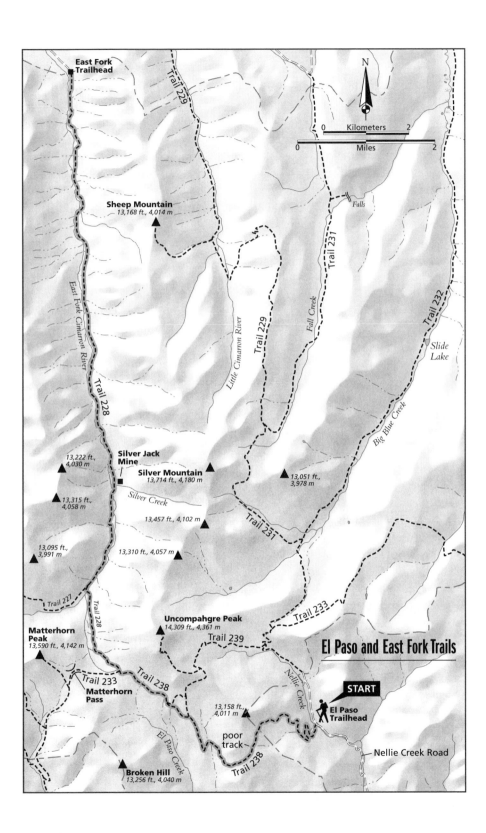

East Fork
Trailhead

Trail 229

N

Kilometers
0   2

Miles
0   2

Falls

Sheep Mountain
13,168 ft., 4,014 m

East Fork Cimarron River

Trail 228

Little Cimarron River

Trail 229

Fall Creek

Trail 231

Trail 232

Slide
Lake

Big Blue Creek

Silver Jack
Mine

13,222 ft.,
4,030 m

Silver Mountain
13,714 ft., 4,180 m

13,051 ft.,
3,978 m

13,315 ft.,
4,058 m

Silver Creek

13,457 ft., 4,102 m

13,095 ft.,
3,991 m

13,310 ft., 4,057 m

Trail 227

Trail 228

Trail 231

Trail 233

Uncompahgre Peak
14,309 ft., 4,361 m

Trail 239

El Paso and East Fork Trails

Matterhorn
Peak
13,590 ft., 4,142 m

Trail 233

Trail 238

START

Nellie Creek

Matterhorn
Pass

13,158 ft.,
4,011 m

El Paso
Trailhead

El Paso Creek

poor
track

Nellie Creek Road

Broken Hill
13,256 ft., 4,040 m

Trail 238

The Hike

This hike is an uncrowded and scenic way to cross the Uncompahgre Wilderness from south to north. Because it starts at the relatively high elevation of 11,200 feet, there is only a moderate amount of uphill hiking involved in reaching the high point of the hike. Views of Uncompahgre, Wetterhorn, and Matterhorn Peaks, Silver Mountain, Sheep Mountain, and the needles of volcanic rock separating the East and Middle Forks of the Cimarron River will keep you entertained as you traverse the Uncompahgre high country.

The first mile of the El Paso Creek Trail (Trail 238) follows an old roadbed and wanders considerably more than is shown on the USGS Uncompahgre Peak quadrangle map. Mild grades, many switchbacks, and three crossings of a small tributary lead to a clearing at about 11,800 feet, below the jagged peak of Point 13,158. The roadbed bends to the northwest, then to the north up the east side of the clearing, reentering the trees. Resist the several informal side trails and stay on the wide roadbed. A short climb leads to a switchback, then to a long traverse southwest below the cliffs of Point 13,158.

You will pass the wilderness boundary sign and timberline at approximately 1.6 miles, and soon after will begin a flat traverse (the general direction is southwest) with fine views of the peaks to the south of Henson Creek. The track may disappear briefly but is easy to pick up again. As the trail bends more to the west, a panorama of (left to right) Broken Hill, Wetterhorn Peak, Matterhorn Peak, and the mass of Uncompahgre Peak develops. Where the terrain begins to drop off more sharply to the west, take a track that stays high and right, and turn toward the northwest into the drainage of El Paso Creek.

The next section of trail loses about 200 feet of elevation as it approaches a tributary (good water source) of El Paso Creek. Take a switchback up the west side of the tributary, and where the trail meets a blunt ridgeline take a hard right. Follow the ridge to where it begins to widen, then break to the northwest—west of the ridge crest—on a faint track at an elevation of approximately 12,100 feet. Follow this across an area of scree, through a rocky area of indistinct topography, and up a short climb to an indistinct drainage divide at just under 12,400 feet. From here drop to the northwest into the drainage of the East Fork, and pick up the East Fork Trail near a point where two drainages converge to form the East Fork. The Ridge Stock Driveway (Trail 233) departs to the west here toward Matterhorn Peak; instead, follow the East Fork Trail (Trail 228) downhill to the north-northwest, parallel to and east of the creek. The track may be faint at first but quickly improves as you drop below 12,000 feet.

Continue dropping into the East Fork Valley and make rapid progress through the highest area of trees. The trail continues down the east side of the river, emerging from the trees and traversing an open hillside before crossing to the west side of the East Fork. Another 0.2 mile leads to a signed trail intersection where a trail (Trail 227) to Middle Fork Pass and the Middle Fork of the Cimarron River departs uphill and to the southwest. Continue instead north and northeast past the intersection, through interspersed meadows and tree cover; the trail becomes faint in one area but is easy to pick up once again. Just before crossing a tributary creek is an area that obviously receives heavy camping use; remember to camp at least 100 feet off the trail if you wish to settle in this area for the night. Once across the tributary make rapid progress to the north and cross the East Fork at a point just above the Silver Jack Mine.

Remains of the Silver Jack Mine include a couple of collapsed buildings and small amounts of mining equipment. This area appears to have been devastated by an avalanche, probably originating high on the west side of the river and spreading its destruction well up onto the east side. Continue north through this area, passing a meadow and heading back into the trees (decent campsites are available near here, with both water sources and tree cover). Below is a stretch where fallen timber and water on the trail may slow progress; large avalanche chutes descend down the opposite (west-side) mountain walls. At about 10,300 feet the trail passes onto the Sheep Mountain quadrangle map. Continue north on a good track; at one point the trail narrows and diverts around an area of heavy fallen timber, but in general there are few obstacles for the next 2 miles. In numerous locations small mudflows have crossed the trail, cutting dramatic channels down the hillside and in places depositing some of their cargo as they cross the trail.

Approximately 2.5 miles from the East Fork Trailhead a tributary drainage is crossed, and at just under a mile from the trailhead is an attractive meadow, but in general the final 3 miles simply proceed down the east side of the East Fork of the Cimarron.

Options

As the El Paso Creek Trail leads into the complex area to the south and southwest of Uncompahgre Peak, there are numerous ways to extend it to create multiday hikes to different trailheads.

31 Uncompahgre Peak and Big Blue Trails
Forest Service Trails 239 and 232

This fine, diverse high-country hike over gentle but high-elevation terrain requires a substantial car shuttle.

Type of hike: Day hike or two-day backpack.
Distance: 12 miles point to point (from the Uncompahgre Trailhead).
16 miles point to point (from the Henson Creek Road).
Difficulty: Moderate.
Trail conditions: The two endpoints of this hike are quite heavily used. The likelihood of solitude is high, however, from the point at

which you leave the Uncompahgre Peak Trail to somewhere near Slide Lake, a distance of about 6 miles. The lower crossing of Big Blue Creek, below Slide Lake, could be difficult or dangerous during periods of high runoff.
Maps: USGS Sheep Mountain and Uncompahgre Peak 7.5-minute quadrangles.
Management: Gunnison Ranger District, Uncompahgre National Forest.

Finding the trailhead: Your starting point for this hike is the Uncompahgre Peak Trailhead, located on the Nellie Creek four-wheel-drive road west of Lake City. In your second vehicle reverse the first Big Blue approach (Alpine Road) described in the previous paragraph, and drive south 11 miles on Colorado Highway 149 to Lake City. From the corner of Second and Gunnison in Lake City, go west on Second Street for two blocks. Turn left at the stop sign onto the Henson Creek Road (Hinsdale County Road 20). At 5.2 miles from Lake City is the well-marked Nellie Creek Road. This point is easily reached in a passenger car, but the Nellie Creek Road requires a high-clearance four-wheel-drive vehicle. Hike, or if possible drive or catch a ride, 3.9 miles to the end of the Nellie Creek Road and the trailhead at about 11,500 feet.

For prehike camping there are abundant campsites available near the Uncompahgre Peak Trailhead, along with a handful of sites along the Henson Creek Road below. Public outhouses are available both at the base of the Nellie Creek Road and at the trailhead. The Big Blue Trailhead has plenty of space for informal camping. The Forest Service's Big Blue Campground, located just a mile to the north of the trailhead, has sanitary facilities.

The end of this hike and shuttle vehicle drop-off will be the Big Blue Trailhead, located just outside the wilderness boundary in the northeastern part of the Uncompahgre. There are two vehicle approaches to Big Blue. The best approach from the Uncompahgre Trailhead is the Alpine Road. From CO 149, 11 miles north of Lake City or 33.6 miles south of the U.S. Highway 50/CO 149 intersection west of Gunnison, turn west onto the Alpine Road. The first 5 miles is narrow and rough but passable in most passenger cars, and leads to an intersection with the Alpine Plateau Road. For the Alpine Plateau Road approach, turn south from U.S. 50, 33.9 miles west of Gunnison and 30.6 miles east of Montrose. The road is also rough but passable in most passenger cars. It forks several times, but signs to Big Blue Campground should help keep you on track. From U.S. 50 it is a slow 21.1 miles to the intersection with the Alpine Road. Whichever approach you prefer, continue northwest from the Alpine Road/Alpine Plateau Road intersection to a small Forest Service building and turn south here (the only option). Pass the Big Blue Campground on the left and reach the trailhead just beyond (a total of 11.9 miles from CO 149, or 27.4 miles from U.S. 50).

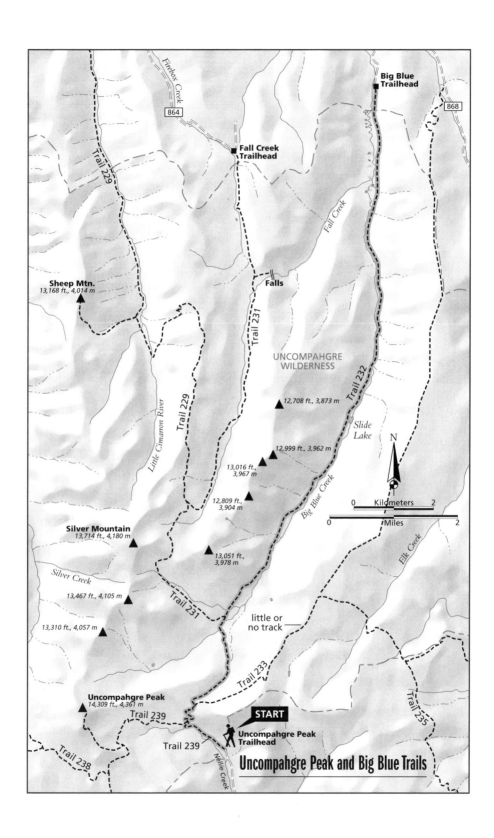

Firebox Creek

864

Trail 229

Fall Creek Trailhead

Big Blue Trailhead

868

Fall Creek

Sheep Mtn.
13,168 ft., 4,014 m

Trail 231

Falls

Little Cimarron River

Trail 229

UNCOMPAHGRE WILDERNESS

12,708 ft., 3,873 m

Trail 232

Slide Lake

12,999 ft., 3,962 m

13,016 ft., 3,967 m

12,809 ft., 3,904 m

Big Blue Creek

N

0   Kilometers   2

0   Miles   2

Silver Mountain
13,714 ft., 4,180 m

13,051 ft., 3,978 m

Silver Creek

13,467 ft., 4,105 m

Elk Creek

13,310 ft., 4,057 m

Trail 231

little or no track

Trail 233

Uncompahgre Peak
14,309 ft., 4,361 m

Trail 235

Trail 239

START

Trail 239

Uncompahgre Peak Trailhead

Nellie Creek

Trail 238

Uncompahgre Peak and Big Blue Trails

Landmarks

0.0 Uncompahgre Trailhead.

0.9 Intersect Big Blue Creek Trail.

1.5 Top of ridge above Big Blue Creek.

3.2 Intersection with Fall Creek Trail.

3.9 Double crossing of Big Blue Creek.

6.8 Slide Lake.

7.8 Crossing of Big Blue Creek.

12.0 Big Blue Trailhead.

The Hike

This two-day through-hike seems to be relatively popular, some parties combining it with an ascent of Uncompahgre Peak. As a two-day overnight trip, it is a relatively easy way to cross the Uncompahgre Wilderness from north to south. If you must hike rather than drive the 3.9 miles up the Nellie Creek Road, it will be a fairly rigorous two days; otherwise the hike is only 12 pleasant miles.

From the Uncompahgre Peak Trailhead, follow Nellie Creek for approximately three-quarters of a mile, where a switchback to the right leads to a junction with the Big Blue Trail (Trail 232). A sign here indicates directions to the Ridge Stock Driveway (Trail 233), the Fall Creek Trail (Trail 231), and the Big Blue Trail. A rising traverse of about 0.2 mile to the northwest leads to a series of switchbacks near the top of the ridge. The saddle just above lies at approximately 12,380 feet. Take heart in the fact that only 1.5 miles from the Uncompahgre Peak Trailhead, you have already reached the high point of the hike.

From the saddle there are two obvious choices. The long traverse to the northeast leads to the northern end of the Ridge Stock Driveway; although an extremely scenic trail, it has no water sources for quite some distance. This hike takes the trail that descends gently into the valley of Big Blue Creek to the north and northeast. The track is obvious as it follows the west bank of a tributary creek for just under a mile to timberline. About 0.6 mile in the trees leads to a large meadow in the picturesque valley of Big Blue Creek. If the track is hard to follow here, just hike to the north-northwest and find the best place to cross the creek. Once on the northwest side of Big Blue Creek, the trail is again easier to find. Follow it for a short distance to the north, where it arrives at a signed intersection with the Fall Creek Trail (Trail 231).

From the intersection with the Fall Creek Trail, it is a pleasant 8.8 miles north and north-northeast to the Big Blue Trailhead. Although there are possible campsites along much of the remainder of the hike, you may wish to continue for a while longer to shorten your second day. About three-quarters of a mile below the junction, the trail descends an open hillside to a creek crossing—or more correctly, a pair of crossings. During low-water conditions you can probably keep your feet dry by tiptoeing along the west bank of the creek for a few hundred feet. Otherwise cross the creek, climb a short hill on the east side, and descend to a second crossing (note that the crossings are not shown accurately on the USGS Uncompahgre Peak quadrangle map). Back on the west side, the trail rises to about 150 feet above the creek for a time; this area has several possible campsites.

About 5 miles south of the Big Blue Trailhead is Slide Lake. Just below the lake you will descend steeply as you cross the massive rockslide that formed the lake. About a mile below Slide Lake is the final creek crossing. During high runoff conditions the crossing could be tricky, but there is no good alternative. Downstream from here the problem is likely to get worse as the Big Blue's streamflow

Uncompahgre Peak from the Ridge Stock Driveway.

increases. Below the crossing the trail passes through a number of small clearings; the hiking is pleasant and easy from here all the way to the trailhead. At about 1.5 miles from the trailhead, you will see Fall Creek dropping into the valley from the west; otherwise there are no significant landmarks. The trailhead lies just beyond the wilderness boundary sign.

Options

There are at least two excellent possibilities for similar but somewhat more strenuous two- to three-day backpacks in this area. From the junction of the Big Blue and Fall Creek Trails, located 3.2 miles from the Uncompahgre Peak Trailhead, you can head once again uphill and west to follow the Fall Creek Trail (Trail 231). This leads to a saddle located at an elevation of approximately 12,700 feet, beyond which is the junction of the Fall Creek and Little Cimarron Trails. The entire route from the Uncompahgre Trailhead to the Fall Creek Trailhead entails 11.4 miles of hiking with about 3,300 feet of elevation gain. The Uncompahgre to Little Cimarron hike is about 15.1 miles in length, with approximately 3,800 feet of elevation gain.

32 Bear Creek Trailhead to Little Elk Trailhead

Forest Service Trails 241, 233, 245, 239, 235, 236, and 244

A diverse multiday, high-country hike that spans the entire Uncompahgre Wilderness from southwest to northeast.

Type of hike: Four- to six-day backpack.
Distance: 36 miles point to point.
Difficulty: Difficult.
Trail conditions: See below.
Maps: USGS Ouray, Ironton, Handies Peak, Wetterhorn Peak, Uncompahgre Peak, Lake City, and Alpine Plateau 7.5-minute quadrangles.
Management: Ouray and Gunnison Ranger Districts, Uncompahgre National Forest.

Finding the trailhead: The hike as described starts at the Bear Creek Trailhead near Ouray. From the southernmost intersection on the main street of Ouray, drive south on U.S. Highway 550 for 2.3 miles, just south of the tunnel, to the trailhead. Parking is available on both sides of the road. There is no space available for trailhead camping. Nearby campsites are located at the USDA Forest Service Amphitheater Campground, just south of Ouray, and dispersed campsites can be found another 6 to 8 miles south on U.S. 550.

You will also likely wish to leave a vehicle or arrange for a pickup at the north end of the Little Elk Trail, where the hike finishes. From Colorado Highway 149, 11 miles north of Lake City or 33.6 miles south of the U.S. 50/CO 149 intersection west of Gunnison, turn west onto the Alpine Road. The Little Elk Trailhead is well marked on the left 3.1 miles up this road, which is rough and narrow but passable by most passenger cars.

It is approximately a two-and-a-half-hour drive between the two trailheads; if you are already in the Lake City area, there is an option to shorten the car shuttle and also the hike. By starting the hike at Engineer Pass, or at the designated Horsethief Trailhead near Engineer Pass, you can limit the shuttle-related driving to approximately 30 miles. In doing so you will also eliminate about 5 miles from the Bear Creek Recreation Trail, including well over 5,500 feet of hiking elevation gain. The eliminated portion of the hike is, however, spectacular and worth the trouble of the long car shuttle.

Trail conditions: Nearly the entire hike lies above timberline and is therefore subject to the vagaries of mountain weather. Several sections of the hike could be difficult to find in the foggy weather that sometimes settles into the San Juan Mountains, and thunderstorm activity is always a possibility during the summer months. Parts of the southern Ridge Stock Driveway and the Little Elk Trail are difficult to find in any conditions, so don't attempt this hike unless you are confident in your route-finding skills. Should weather or anything else cause you to shorten the hike, however, there are many opportunities to bail off the high ridges and into the drainages on the periphery of the Uncompahgre via other established trails. Hiking some of these connecting trails (particularly those with trailheads along Henson Creek and North Henson Creek, which can provide a quick escape) will improve your familiarity with the terrain you cross. The connecting trails include the Uncompahgre Peak Trail (Hike 21), Matterhorn Peak Trail (Hike 22), Matterhorn Cutoff (Hike 24), and Mary Alice Creek (Hike 25).

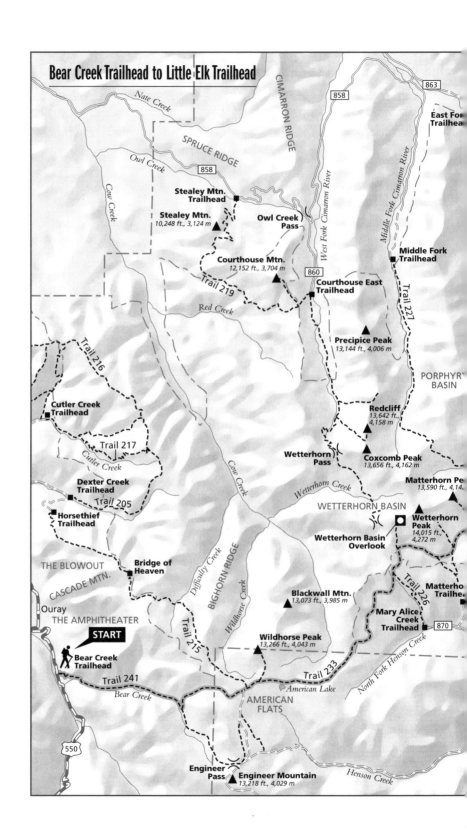

Bear Creek Trailhead to Little Elk Trailhead

Stealey Mtn. Trailhead

Stealey Mtn.
10,248 ft., 3,124 m

Owl Creek Pass

Courthouse Mtn.
12,152 ft., 3,704 m

Courthouse East Trailhead

Middle Fork Trailhead

East For Trailhea

Precipice Peak
13,144 ft., 4,006 m

PORPHYR
BASIN

Cutler Creek Trailhead

Trail 217

Redcliff
13,642 ft., 4,158 m

Wetterhorn Pass

Coxcomb Peak
13,656 ft., 4,162 m

Dexter Creek Trailhead

Trail 205

Matterhorn Pe
13,590 ft., 4,14.

Horsethief Trailhead

WETTERHORN BASIN

Wetterhorn Peak
14,015 ft., 4,272 m

Wetterhorn Basin Overlook

THE BLOWOUT

CASCADE MTN.

Bridge of Heaven

Blackwall Mtn.
13,073 ft., 3,985 m

Matterho Trailhe.

Ouray
THE AMPHITHEATER

START

Mary Alice Creek Trailhead

870

Trail 226

Bear Creek Trailhead

Trail 241

Bear Creek

Wildhorse Peak
13,266 ft., 4,043 m

Trail 233

American Lake

AMERICAN FLATS

550

Engineer Pass

Engineer Mountain
13,218 ft., 4,029 m

Henson Creek

Nate Creek

SPRUCE RIDGE

Owl Creek

858

Cow Creek

Trail 219

Red Creek

Trail 216

Cutler Creek

Cow Creek

Difficulty Creek

BIGHORN RIDGE

Wildhorse Creek

Trail 215

North Fork Henson Creek

Cimarron Ridge

858

863

West Fork Cimarron River

Middle Fork Cimarron River

860

Wetterhorn Creek

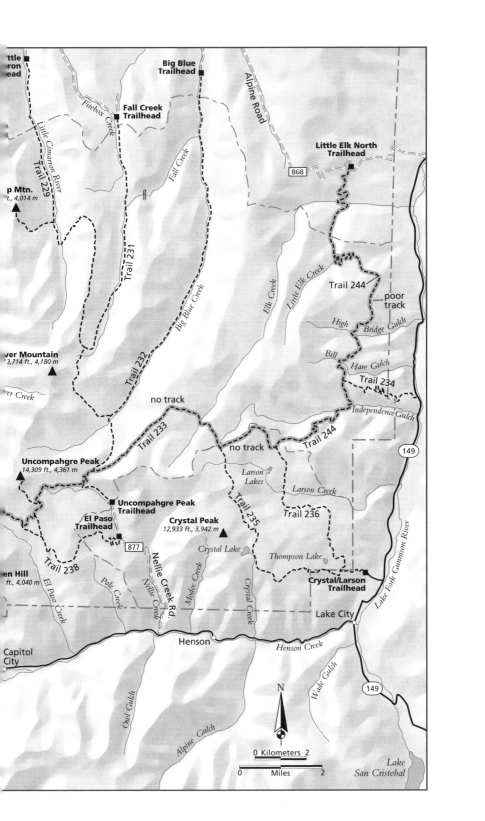

ttle
ron
ead

Big Blue
Trailhead

Fall Creek
Trailhead

Firebox Creek

Little Cimarron River

Trail 229

p Mtn.
t., 4,014 m

Trail 231

Fall Creek

Alpine Road

Little Elk North
Trailhead

868

Trail 244

poor
track

High

Bridge Gulch

Bill

Hare Gulch

Trail 234

Independence Gulch

Elk Creek

Little Elk Creek

er Mountain
3,714 ft., 4,180 m

er Creek

Trail 232

Big Blue Creek

no track

Trail 233

no track

Trail 244

149

Uncompahgre Peak
14,309 ft., 4,361 m

Uncompahgre Peak
Trailhead

El Paso
Trailhead

Crystal Peak
12,933 ft., 3,942 m

Trail 235

*Larson
Lakes*

Larson Creek

Trail 236

877

Trail 238

n Hill
ft., 4,040 m

El Paso Creek

Pole Creek

Nellie Creek Rd.

Nellie Creek

Motoc Creek

Crystal Lake

Crystal Creek

Thompson Lake

Crystal/Larson
Trailhead

Lake Fork Gunnison River

Lake City

Capitol
City

Henson

Henson Creek

Out Gulch

Alpine Gulch

Wade Gulch

149

N

0 Kilometers 2

0   Miles   2

*Lake
San Cristobal*

Although many sections of the hike feel very isolated, you will rarely be more than 5 miles from the nearest trailhead and civilization. This hike stays at high elevations for long periods and requires a very high degree of fitness.

There are relatively few areas along the length of this hike where sheltered (tree-protected) campsites and water sources are available; the best of these are listed below.

Yellowjacket Mine 3.6 miles

American Lake (water, no shelter) 7.1 miles

Mary Alice Creek 12 miles

Matterhorn Creek 14.1 miles

Nellie Creek (water, poor shelter) 19.6 miles

Elk Creek 23.5 miles

Independence Gulch 28.2 miles

It is recommended that you choose your period to hike this route with stable weather and water availability in mind. If you pick a stretch of stormy weather, the hike will be miserable and very possibly dangerous as well, so try to avoid the late-July and August monsoon season. Going too late in the year may also mean the drying up of numerous marginal water sources at high elevations. It would seem, then, that the ideal time for this hike, at least in a "normal" year, might be during a clear period in late June or early July. Whenever possible, plan your days around reaching locations with tree cover in early to midafternoon in case thunderstorms do develop. Avoid areas such as American Flats, the southeast ridge of Uncompahgre Peak, and the high ridge of the northern Ridge Stock Driveway when weather is threatening.

Landmarks

0.0 Bear Creek Trailhead.

2.5 Cross tributary of Bear Creek.

3.6 Yellowjacket Mine.

5.6 Ridgetop above American Flats

6.3 Junction with Horsethief Trail and Ridge Stock Driveway; continue east.

11.9 Junction with Mary Alice Creek Trail; continue north.

12.7 Junction with trail to Wetterhorn Basin Overlook; turn right (east).

14.1 Junction with Matterhorn Creek Trail; turn left (east).

15.4 Matterhorn Pass.

16.7 Intersect East Fork Trail; turn right (east).

18.0 Southeast ridge of Uncompahgre Peak.

20.0 Intersect Uncompahgre Peak Trail to Nellie Creek Trailhead; turn left (north).

20.4 Junction with Big Blue Trail; turn right (east).

21.9 Point 12,805 on Ridge Stock Driveway.

23.6 Join Crystal Lake Trail (Trail 235).

24.4 Join Larson Lakes Trail (Trail 236); turn left (northeast).

26.1 Join Little Elk Trail (Trail 244); turn left (north).

28.2 Cross Independence Gulch.

29.0 Junction with Independence Trail (Trail 234); turn left (north).

36.0 Little Elk North Trailhead.

The Hike

This hike represents only one of many possibilities presented by the Uncompahgre Wilderness for multiday backcountry adventures. It traverses the entire area from southwest to northeast, mostly via the spectacular Ridge Stock Driveway (Trail 233). The hike involves some route-finding difficulties, as it begins up a deep canyon near Ouray and travels over high-country ridges, then finally into the more subdued foothills terrain north of Lake City.

You will begin on the Bear Creek National Recreation Trail (Trail 241). The Bear Creek Trailhead is located just south of the tunnel. Cross above the tunnel and negotiate numerous switchbacks up the mountainside. Cross the top of the slate scree slope and continue across a ledge leading uphill and south. As the trail begins to turn the corner into the drainage of Bear Creek at about 0.9 mile, Red Mountain to the south and the Sneffels Range to the west come progressively into view. The next half mile passes under several 300-foot cliffs that are subject to rockfall. Move as quickly as possible through these sections. For perhaps a half mile, the trail follows ledges 200 feet or so above the creek, with some very steep drops below. Drop down and right across a tributary drainage at approximately 2.5 miles, and proceed to the east. Follow steeper grades on a very pleasant trail to the remains of the Yellowjacket Mine at about 3.6 miles. This area has the last tree-sheltered campsites for a great distance, so finding an excuse to knock off might be easy.

From the Yellowjacket Mine hike south-southeast on a well-marked trail into the southern of the two drainages that come together in the area of the mine. You will soon reach a trail junction with a sign indicating the direction and distance back to U.S. 550; turn left onto a trail heading north and northeast up a steady grade. Make an easy stream crossing, then follow what may be an old roadbed for about 0.3 mile into the upper basin above tree line. The trail may become faint, but try to trend northeast, then east until it becomes obvious again. Continue generally east toward the obvious low point (also the wilderness area boundary) on the ridge ahead. From this saddle follow switchbacks downhill into American Flats, basking in the views of the Uncompahgre's high peaks to the northeast. Continue east-northeast to a three-way trail intersection near the base of Wildhorse Peak's south slopes.

From the three-way trail junction, hike (now on the Ridge Stock Driveway, Trail 233) east and pick up a good track, which passes just north of American Lake. You are now approximately 7 miles from the Bear Creek Trailhead, and camping near this water source may seem like a good idea. Fill all containers here in any case, as the next reliable water source is Mary Alice Creek, about 5 miles distant. Continue east of American Lake on a flat to slightly downhill grade on a northwest-facing hillside, just above the headwaters of Cow Creek. About 1.8 miles past American Lake, the

Scenery along the southern Ridge Stock Driveway.

trail crosses the ridgeline north of Point 12,368 (leaving the wilderness area) and enters a small drainage. Note that the short trail shown on the Trails Illustrated map leading into this area from the upper end of North Henson Creek (from the southeast) is no longer in existence, as it is located on private land. From the drainage follow a poor track to the north-northeast—not through the deepest drainage below south-facing cliffs but through a smaller drainage to the south—to another small saddle.

The next 2 miles of trail is poorly defined and should not be attempted without map and compass in hand or if visibility is limited. From the saddle described above, climb a short, steep hillside to the west and descend north and northeast into a broad basin. In the absence of a clear track, follow your instincts, staying at an elevation near 12,000 feet all the way to the drainage (water source except during dry conditions) that lies directly southwest of Mary Alice Creek. A good track leads uphill out of this drainage, over a ridgeline about a half mile northwest of Point 12,334, then gently downhill into the drainage of Mary Alice Creek. Good campsites and water are available at Mary Alice Creek, or feel free to push on toward Matterhorn Creek, another 2 miles distant. Escape is possible to the south (to the North Henson Creek Road) from here via the Mary Alice Creek Trail (Trail 226).

From the intersection with the Mary Alice Creek Trail, a network of braided trails (possibly game trails) leads north to a 12,460-foot saddle just to the west of Point 12,547 and reentry into the Uncompahgre Wilderness (a small sign marks the boundary). For the next 6 miles, you will be treated to views of the Uncompahgre's highest peaks. Hike north from the saddle, downhill through a trough of sorts, and meet the upper end of Matterhorn Creek. The Matterhorn Cutoff (Trail 245) lacks a good track as it follows the north side of the creek downstream for about three-quarters of a mile. As the terrain steepens you will pick up a better trail. Just past (east of) an area of willows, the trail splits; take the left fork toward Wetterhorn and Matterhorn Peaks. You will meet up with the Matterhorn Peak Trail (Trail 233) about 0.4 mile past the trail split. Below and adjacent to the Matterhorn Peak Trail are some very nice tree-sheltered campsites with water. After passing through so much dry terrain above timberline, it may be hard to resist spending the night in this area. Escape to the North Henson Creek Road is easy from here via the Matterhorn Creek Trail and the Matterhorn Road.

To proceed east from Matterhorn Creek, head north and northeast on Trail 233. Crank up a steep ridge between two small drainages, and hike 0.7 mile or so on much easier ground to the 12,458-foot saddle (referred to here as Matterhorn Pass) southeast of Matterhorn Peak. From here the highest summits of the Uncompahgre (Wetterhorn, Matterhorn, Uncompahgre, and numerous only slightly lower peaks) are in full view. The trail descends slightly to the east from the saddle. There is no need to take the horseshoe-shaped 300-foot uphill diversion to the south as shown on both the USGS and Trails Illustrated maps; rather, continue downhill to the east and northeast to where the drainage splits (this is the headwaters of the East Fork of the Cimarron River). The East Fork Trail (Trail 228) departs from here to the northwest and downhill. To continue, climb briefly to the east on a good track and proceed to the east-southeast below the hulking southwest face of Uncompahgre Peak. Pass through some hummocky terrain and look for a good trail that cuts left just before a scree-covered area. Take this left-hand trail, then hike uphill to the northeast to connect with a track that angles uphill toward the southeast shoulder of Uncompahgre Peak. When you reach the shoulder, you will be on the Uncompahgre Peak Trail (Trail 239), where you may encounter more people than on the rest of the hike put together.

From the shoulder of Uncompahgre, you will descend the Uncompahgre Peak Trail for about 1.3 miles. The trail is obvious as it loses almost 1,000 feet of elevation over this distance. Just before descending an embankment is a sign indicating directions to the Ridge Stock Driveway and other trails. Just below is Nellie Creek, with sheltered campsites, easy escape to the Henson Creek Road, and an opportunity to fill your water containers; the next reliable water supply is close to 4 miles ahead. From the signed trail intersection, hike up the switchbacks to the north toward the Ridge Stock Driveway (Trail 233). A 12,380-foot saddle at the top of this climb presents the appealing traverse to the northeast on the Ridge Stock Driveway. For the first mile of this traverse, you will neither gain nor lose significant elevation. The traverse yields unobstructed views of Silver Mountain's mass across the valley of Big Blue Creek to the northwest as well as behind you to Uncompahgre Peak. At the traverse's end a switchback to the south and a 300-foot climb will deposit you on top of the long, gentle ridge that makes up the north end of the Ridge Stock Driveway. Note the presence of a marker post with a base of stacked rocks; if you end up having to retreat from the ridge, this is the spot at which to descend. This ridge holds a powerful draw, as it is by far the dominant feature in the eastern third of the Uncompahgre Wilderness.

There is no discernible track heading north along the ridgetop, but the way is clear; stay on or near the topographic high as you proceed to the northeast. You will hike only slightly uphill to an elaborate cairn or windbreak on top of Point 12,805. From there a very gradual descent allows rapid progress. About a mile past the high point, keep an eye out for a trail rounding a hillside below and to the east (right); this is the Crystal Lake Trail (Trail 235) as it enters the drainage of Elk Creek. You will need to connect up with Trail 235 from the Ridge Stock Driveway; although both the USGS Uncompahgre Peak quadrangle and the Trails Illustrated map show the trails coming together more than 2 miles ahead, it will be very difficult to resist the impulse to simply descend the gentle hillside below. Fill water containers if necessary from Elk Creek, and proceed around the corner to the east on the Crystal Lake Trail.

A good trail climbs steeply, first to the south then back east and northeast, from Elk Creek. After climbing about 400 feet in less than a half mile, pass over a ridgetop and traverse to the southeast on more level ground. Cross a small drainage (the uppermost part of Independence Gulch) and find a trail intersection at the edge of a large, very featureless plateau. From the trail junction turn onto the Larson Lakes Trail (Trail 236). Hike east-northeast across the plateau; there is only a poor track, if any, but several prominent marker posts indicate the way. You will be essentially following the wilderness boundary, and at the northeastern end of the plateau is a boundary sign. Descend to the north past some small rock outcrops and a couple of switchbacks, then drop below timberline. The trail becomes wide and quite easy to follow as it loops downhill to the east, southeast, and finally to the south. You will very quickly come upon a flat area with a trail branching to the northeast; this is the Little Elk Trail (Trail 244), the final (but still rather long) leg of the hike. About 500 feet down the Little Elk from the trail junction is the wilderness boundary once again (here you are entering the Uncompahgre, though it's not immediately obvious whether you are leaving or entering).

From the boundary a corridor through the trees leads north, then generally northeast down a steady grade. Bend more to the east as you enter the drainage of Independence Gulch, still steadily downhill. In places the track is faint, but it can be followed with the help of occasional tree blazes. Pass a short, steep downhill, a small clearing, and a switchback to a larger clearing. Hike northeast past a marker post in the clearing, then bear slightly uphill and left past another post rather than continuing down the drainage. Tree blazes mark the way if you look carefully.

The trail will now trend more north and downhill, and you will soon hear the sound of water. Hike parallel to Independence Gulch for a few hundred feet; good campsites with available water can be found in this area. At a switchback the trail crosses the creek; fill water containers here if necessary, as it is more than 2 miles to the next reliable source. On the northeast side of the creek, find an indistinct track (if it exists at all) heading east–northeast up a grassy hillside. Follow this for 300 to 400 feet and drop to a crossing to the north side of a small tributary drainage. Intersect a trail with a small sign indicating the direction back to the Larson Lakes Trail. Note that if you wish to hasten the end of your outing, going right and downhill on this trail leads to a water diversion ditch and a relatively easy trip out to the Independence Trailhead. To stay on the Little Elk Trail, you will instead go left and up a moderately steep grade for approximately 0.2 mile to a clearing. Stay to the right (east or northeast) side of the clearing as you hike uphill, following marker posts. Near the upper end of the clearing, pick up a better trail as it reenters the trees. Pass through beautiful mature aspen groves, hiking generally in a northerly direction. As you approach Bill Hare Gulch, you will intersect the Independence Trail (Trail 234) at a signed junction. From here an easy downhill escape (definitely recommended for those who are uncertain of their navigational skills) via Trail 234 to the Independence Trailhead is possible (see the descriptions under Hikes 17 and 18 in this book). The finish described here continues (with some route-finding difficulty) to the north end of the Little Elk Trail.

The final section of the hike will involve about 7 miles of moderate hiking to the northern trailhead of the Little Elk. The route finding on this last section is very challenging, so be prepared with map and compass and the skills to use them. Hike briefly uphill to the north, then begin dropping into Bill Hare Gulch. Hike uphill to the west, then cross a small drainage and an open slope back to the northeast. Descend back to the northwest, cross Bill Hare Gulch, and crank a 200-foot climb up the open north side of the valley below some rock outcrops. Cross a ridgetop and descend northeast and north into High Bridge Gulch. You will enter a small meadow where the trail may disappear; continue downhill past a stand of aspen on the left to an open, rounded, northeast-trending divide. From here a better trail is once again visible, cutting northwest back into the trees.

A long, gentle descent to the northwest leads to a tributary of High Bridge Gulch; climb out its north side and continue to the north through a fantastic aspen grove. If you lose the trail here, simply find the ridge that separates the tributary from High Bridge Gulch, then hike to the west along its top until you find the trail dropping to the northwest off the ridge. Follow this across High Bridge, and begin the long gradual climb out the north side of the gulch on an open hillside. At the top of this grade (you are now just across the map boundary, onto the USGS Alpine Plateau quadrangle, southeast of Point 11,110), turn to the north into a very small drainage. Proceed north-northwest through aspen, then turn more to the northeast on an open hillside. A short climb across this leads to an east-facing hillside of aspen groves interspersed with meadows.

The next 1.5 miles of the trail may be very difficult to follow, but the idea (follow along with this description on the USGS Alpine Plateau quadrangle) is to wind up on a saddle located about 1.7 miles to the northwest, just north of the Hinsdale–Gunnison County line, just south of the cliffs below Point 10,393, and just east of Little Elk Creek. On the map the saddle elevation is shown as 10,064 feet. The cliffs can be seen from a number of places along this portion of the trail, so keep them in mind as a landmark. Once in the east-facing meadow, hike north-northeast, losing elevation only slightly. At the north end of the meadow, look for a break in a fence line and follow a better trail through the trees. At a second large meadow, the trail is likely to disappear again. Descend and traverse to the north-northeast, looking for a marker post at the north end of the clearing. If the post and trail are not found, the next section can be negotiated (I proved this the hard way) via a series of game trails. If you are able to find the trail, follow it mostly downhill and northwest, around the upper end of Well Gulch, aiming for the small clearings visible on the map to the southeast of Point 10,393. If you lose the trail, be careful not to lose any more elevation than necessary as you progress to the northwest into Well Gulch. As you enter the clearing between Well Gulch and the 10,064-foot saddle, hike west and up a mild grade past a couple of marker posts, through an area of aspen, and around the south, southwest, and west sides of a second, larger clearing. The trail is faint to nonexistent but will improve as you make the final climb via switchbacks to the saddle.

Still on the saddle, hike southwest briefly into the trees and begin descending on a good trail into the drainage of Little Elk Creek. The descent is gradual, using numerous switchbacks, and in a surprisingly short time you will cross to the west side of the creek. The next 1.3 miles mainly parallels Little Elk Creek downstream, with a short section crossing to the east side then back to the west. You will continue to lose elevation rapidly here. Cross back to the east side once again, pass a muddy section of about 0.2 mile, then cross Little Elk Creek for the last time at a muddy area. Hiking approximately 0.2 mile upstream and parallel to Elk Creek leads to a crossing and to the final uphill push.

Ascend the hillside to the north of Elk Creek in a series of switchbacks, then follow a blunt divide uphill and across the Thompson No. 2 irrigation ditch. Cross an open hillside, then descend briefly through trees to a meadow just above a fence line and the ditch. Follow a small drainage uphill (the trail may be very faint here) for approximately 0.1 mile, then climb a hillside to the right (north), pass through an area of aspen, and emerge within sight of the trailhead. If the last portion of the trail is lost, following the fence line will lead to a point on the Alpine Road about 0.2 mile below the trailhead.

Options

If you wish to stretch this adventure even more, an alternative start is the Horsethief Trail (Trail 215)), which starts in the Dexter Creek drainage north of Ouray (see Hike 2). This option adds about 4 miles and another 500 feet of elevation gain to the hike. Since the hike as described traverses the entire Uncompahgre Wilderness, many variations are possible.

Appendix

Trail Finder

Easy Day Hikes

1. Bear Creek National Recreation Trail to Yellowjacket Mine, Forest Service Trail 241
5. Storm Gulch to Baldy Peak, Forest Service Trails 212 and 216.1A
6. Baldy Trail to Baldy Peak, Forest Service Trail 216.1A
7. Stealey Mountain Trail to Stealey Mountain, Forest Service Trail 219
9. Courthouse Mountain, Forest Service Trail 218
25. Mary Alice Creek and Matterhorn Cutoff to Matterhorn Trailhead, Forest Service Trails 226 and 245
26. Engineer Pass to American Flats and Wildhorse Peak

Moderate Day Hikes

2. Horsethief Trail to Bridge of Heaven, Forest Service Trail 215
3. Dexter Creek Trail, Forest Service Trail 205
4. Cutler Creek Loop, Forest Service Trails 217 and 217.2A
8. Courthouse and Stealey Mountain Trails, Forest Service Trails 218 and 219
10. Point 13,241
12. Wetterhorn Basin Trail to Wetterhorn Pass, Forest Service Trail 226
15. Fall Creek Trail, Forest Service Trail 231
16. Big Blue Trail to Slide Lake and Beyond, Forest Service Trail 232
21. Uncompahgre Peak Trail, Forest Service Trail 239
22. Matterhorn Peak, Forest Service Trail 233
24. Matterhorn Cutoff to Wetterhorn Basin Overlook, Forest Service Trails 233 and 245

Difficult Day Hikes

1. Bear Creek National Recreation Trail, American Flats loop
11. Redcliff
12. Wetterhorn Basin Trail to Wetterhorn Basin, Forest Service Trail 226
13. Middle Fork Trail to Middle Fork Pass, Forest Service Trail 227
14. Little Cimarron Trail to Sheep Mountain, Forest Service Trail 229
17. Little Elk and Independence Trails, Forest Service Trails 244 and 234
18. Larson Lakes, Little Elk, and Independence Trails, Forest Service Trails 236, 244, and 234
19. Larson Lakes and Crystal Lake Loop, Forest Service Trails 236 and 235
20. El Paso Creek Trail to Uncompahgre Peak, Forest Service Trails 238, 233, and 239
23. Wetterhorn Peak, Forest Service Trail 233

Backpack Trips (from Easiest to Most Difficult)

31. Uncompahgre Peak and Big Blue Trails, Forest Service Trails 239 and 232
29. Fall Creek and Little Cimarron Trails, Forest Service Trails 231 and 229
28. Middle Fork and East Fork Trails, Forest Service Trails 227 and 228
30. El Paso and East Fork Trails, Forest Service Trails 238 and 228
27. Bear Creek National Recreation Trail to American Flats and Horsethief Trail, Forest Service Trails 241 and 215
32. Bear Creek Trailhead to Little Elk Trailhead, Forest Service Trails 241, 233, 245, 239, 235, 236, and 244

About the Author

Author Bill Crick grew up in western Pennsylvania, and from a very young age had a mysterious attraction to mountainous places. He fell in love with Colorado at age twelve during a trip west with his parents ("We wanted to show him some real mountains"), and he landed in the state for good at age twenty-four. Bill has spent the intervening two decades, most of it with his wife Cathy, escaping the flatlands at every opportunity to hike and climb in the Colorado high country. Bill and Cathy currently live in Denver but are plotting an escape from the city to a place offering easier access to the mountains.

What's So Special about Unspoiled, Natural Places?

Beauty Solitude Wildness Freedom Quiet Adventure

Serenity Inspiration Wonder Excitement

Relaxation Challenge

There's a lot to love about our treasured public lands, and the reasons are different for each of us. Whatever your reasons are, the national **Leave No Trace** education program will help you discover special outdoor places, enjoy them, and preserve them—today and for those who follow. By practicing and passing along these simple principles, you can help protect the special places you love from being loved to death.

The Principles of Leave No Trace

- Plan ahead and prepare
- Travel and camp on durable surfaces
- Dispose of waste properly
- Leave what you find
- Minimize campfire impacts
- Respect wildlife
- Be considerate of other visitors

Leave No Trace is a national nonprofit organization dedicated to teaching responsible outdoor recreation skills and ethics to everyone who enjoys spending time outdoors.

To learn more or to become a member, please visit us at www.LNT.org or call (800) 332-4100.

Leave No Trace, P.O. Box 997, Boulder, CO 80306